Rose Johnson

W9-ARM-489

THE SMART APPROACH TO

WINDOW DECOR

CREATIVE
HOMEOWNER®

THE SMART APPROACH TO
WINDOW DECOR

Lynn Elliott & Lisa Lent

CREATIVE HOMEOWNER®, Upper Saddle River, New Jersey

COPYRIGHT © 2000

CRE▲TIVE
HOMEOWNER®

A Division of Federal Marketing Corp.
Upper Saddle River, NJ

This book may not be reproduced, either in part or in its entirety, in any form by any means, without written permission from the publisher; with the exception of brief excerpts for purposes of radio, television, or published review. Although all possible measures have been taken to ensure the accuracy of the material presented, neither the author nor the publisher is liable in case of misinterpretation of directions, misapplication, or typographical error. All rights, including the right of translation, are reserved.

Editorial Director: Timothy O. Bakke
Art Director: W. David Houser
Production Manager: Ann Bernstein

Authors: Lynn Elliott, Lisa Lent
Senior Editor, Decorating Books: Kathie Robitz
Book Editor & Photo Researcher: Lynn Elliott
Contributing Writer: Anne Marie Soto

Graphic Designers: Glee Barre, Susan Hallinan
Layout: Virginia Wells Blaker
Illustrator: Barbara Griffel
Templates Illustrator: Tina Basile

Cover Design: Susan Hallinan
Cover Photography: Gordon Beall
Back Cover Photography: Steve Gross &
Susan Daley (top left); Mark Lohman (top
right and bottom left)

Current Printing (last digit)
10 9 8 7

The Smart Approach to Window Decor,
First Edition
Library of Congress Catalog Card Number: 99-64943
ISBN: 1-58011-071-1

CREATIVE HOMEOWNER®
A Division of Federal Marketing Corp.
24 Park Way
Upper Saddle River, NJ 07458

Web Site: **www.creativehomeowner.com**

Acknowledgments

Sincere thanks to all of those who generously offered their assistance, especially the staffs at Windows of Montclair and Country Curtains as well as the American Society of Interior Designers (ASID). Recognition must also go to Anne Marie Soto for her contribution. On a personal note, a special thank you to Dolores and John Elliott for their unfailing support.

Contents

Introduction   8

Chapter One
The Role of Window Treatments   12

A window treatment plays an important part in the home. It provides privacy, controls light, and frames a view. This chapter also examines its significance as a decorative element.

Chapter Two
What's Your Window Style?   20

A discussion about how to identify the style of your window and how that influences your choices for window decor. All the information you need to successfully pick out the appropriate design.

Chapter Three
What's Your Decor?   30

Now is the time to start thinking about how to enhance the overall style of your room with the right window dressing. This chapter will guide you through the decision-making process.

Chapter Four
Lifestyle & Budget   38

Here you'll find practical guidelines to consider when selecting a window arrangement, including whether or not to go the custom route by hiring an interior designer.

Chapter Five
Curtains & Draperies   48

An overview of all types of curtains and draperies, including gathered, pleated, tabbed, plain, and pierced styles. Plus, how to choose linings, curtain lengths, and tieback positions.

Chapter Six
Shades, Blinds & Shutters   66

A review of the range of styles for shades, blinds, and shutters. Learn how to decide the best way to install your treatment, as well as how to choose a hem design for shades.

Chapter Seven
Cornices, Valances & Swags   84

Cornices, valances, and swags can finish off the top of a window arrangement or stand alone. Topics include pulling together formal or informal looks with these versatile top treatments.

Chapter Eight
Choosing a Fabric   102

A guide to selecting the right fabric for your window dressing—from cottons and linens to velvets and tapestries. Plus, this chapter shows you how to mix patterns.

Chapter Nine
Decorative Embellishments   110

Tassels, trimmings, rosettes, and tiebacks are a way to add a distinctive touch to a window treatment. Learn to bring out the best in your design with these decorative accents.

Chapter Ten
Drapery Hardware   122

More than just functional, drapery hardware can be decorative. Let this chapter show you why—and how—to incorporate it into your overall design.

Chapter Eleven
Problem Solving   132

Some windows are a challenge to dress. They can be too big, too small, and oddly shaped. Find solutions for common problems such as corner windows, special shapes, and dormer units.

Chapter Twelve
Make Your Own Curtains   146

If you're handy with sewing projects, this chapter reviews some easy steps for making your own curtains, swags, and decorative embellishments. Includes how to measure your window.

Appendix   154

Glossary   170

Index   172

Introduction

S electing the right window treatment can be confusing. There are so many things to consider: the architecture of the window; the style of the room; your lifestyle and budget; and how you want the window treatment to look and function. And like any other aspect of good design, dressing a window takes a concentrated effort to get it right. That's how *The Smart Approach to Window Decor* can help you.

By presenting a wide range of window-treatment types and styles, the book provides lots of ideas that can inspire your own design. But more than that, *The Smart Approach to Window Decor* walks you through the decision-making process, step by step. It helps you to see the "big picture," first by analyzing the structure of the window and its place within the architecture. Then it shows you how to take that information and study it alongside the other decorative elements of your home, such as the furnishings. Once you've mastered that, you'll be ready to tackle the questions of lifestyle and budget, which should help you decide whether or not to go the custom route. "Smart Tips" scattered throughout the book offer handy decorator advice, too.

Whichever kind you choose, custom window treatments or ready-made ones, you'll find the chapters that explore the various types of coverings—curtains and draperies, shades, blinds, and shutters, and cornices, valances, and swags—

The style and fabrics used to make this layered window treatment underscore the traditional look of this living room.

Formal curtains, *above, add grandeur to a small room.*

Simplicity *allows the beautiful architecture of these windows, right, to stand out.*

insightful, particularly when they are combined with the advice for choosing a fabric. If you're looking for a way to add flair to your design, you'll find that the discussion of the various types of decorative embellishments will show you how to add rich details. When you're ready to install your new window treatment, a review of functional and decorative hardware, starting on page 122, will explain how to select the right type of mounting device.

Some types of windows are challenging to dress because of their size, shape, or locations. Chapter 11, "Problem Solving," which begins on page 132, offers solutions to many of the most common problems homeowners face when challenged with an awkward window placement. If you're handy with sewing projects, you'll find instructions for creating your own curtains, swags, and embellishments in Chapter 12, "Make Your Own Curtains," beginning on page 146.

A soft shade, above, adjusts for daytime reading.

An informal valance, above right, puts a contemporary face on a period room.

Fresh colors, right, perk up a neutral scheme.

Finally, if you want to play with a few different looks before making up your mind, consult the Appendix. Scaled versions of various window types and numerous window-treatment styles let you try out a variety of designs so that you can see what they may look like in your home.

The Smart Approach to Window Decor should make choosing a window treatment easy and creative—no more worrying about costly mistakes. You can use it alone or take it along if you're consulting a professional designer. With this book in hand, there are no more excuses for leaving windows bare.

The Role of Window Treatments

A penniless post-Civil War Scarlett O'Hara wore hers, silk bullion fringe and all, but that's not what comes to mind for most people when considering the purpose of window treatments. Haute couture aside, curtains, shades, and blinds can serve a variety of purposes in the home. Some of these functions are practical; others are purely decorative. Because most window treatments have this versatility, they are important elements in any design.

When you think of the role a window treatment may play in your plans, consider a number of factors. Do you need a way to control sunlight and glare? Can you use the window treatment to limit heat gain during the summer or heat loss during the winter? Do you want to obscure an undesirable view? Are you looking for a way to create privacy? Can you use a window treatment to modify or enhance the architectural elements of the space? Can you use it to bring color, pattern, or texture into a room?

Of course, the right window treatment can do any of these things. But it can also establish or underscore a decorative style, whether it is contemporary, traditional, country, or period. On a large window or one that is situated prominently, the right dressing can also create a focal point in a space that lacks this important visual anchor.

*A **cloud-like effect** of billowing fabric softens the geometry of the individual double-hung windows in this bay and ties them together as one treatment.*

Form Follows Function

Today, there is a wide selection of window treatments and materials to address any or all of these concerns. Because conditions of light, heat, and lifestyle dictate changes over the course of the day or even from season to season, it's wise to select a style that is easily adjustable. For example, natural light that streams over your shoulder, while you sit in a chair with your back to the window, is lovely for reading a book. However, if you're working at a computer that is in the direct path of harsh sunlight, the glare caused by the sun's reflection on the monitor will make it difficult to read what's on the screen and may strain your eyes. A window covering that can be lowered or closed at will allows you to enjoy natural light when you want it or close it out when you don't.

Before getting started on your window-decor project, go over the following steps to make sure you're contemplating a window treatment that does the job you need it to do.

One: ***Consider ventilation and airflow.*** Sometimes you'll want to open your windows to let in fresh air and release indoor pollutants. And on occasion, you may prefer a natural breeze to an air conditioner. So choose a covering that won't impede the flow of air into the room. On the other hand, if the windows are a source for draughts or heat collection, consider specially insulated curtains that can cut down on these problems and may even save you the cost of replacing old windows.

Two: ***Examine the sight lines.*** What is the first thing you see when you enter a room? In most cases, it is the windows. Can you see them from outside the entry? You know what they say about first impressions, so use the window treatments to make an immediate style statement.

Three: ***Look out, look in.*** Do you want to take in the view? Then, you may want minimal window dressing. But what about privacy? You won't like the feeling that you're living in a fishbowl, especially at night when all you can see is a black hole to the outside, while your neighbors can watch your every move. A treatment that's adjustable, such as curtains, shades, or blinds that open and close

Elegant swag-and-jabot valances, left, pair with floor-length curtains to create a harmonious bridge between a window, the wall, and a French door.

Single, floor-length panels, right, sidestep an awkwardly situated radiator in front of a bank of windows. A matching valance lends more formality while adjustable venetian blinds let in or block out light as desired.

For privacy that doesn't sacrifice light and ventilation in this bathroom, the designer recommended a bottom-mounted shade. The valance adds a soft, pretty touch.

Five: **Look at the room's general decor.** Does it appear tired, dated, or simply unfinished? Consider how new window treatments can put a fresh face on the room.

THE PRACTICAL ROLE OF A WINDOW TREATMENT

When you imagine heavy, multi-layered fabric covering a window, it's usually in a period- or historic-design context. (Although lighter-weight versions are popular in traditional homes, today.) Textiles, such as lined wool, damask, silk, brocade, velvet, and tapestries, provided much-needed insulation against extreme temperatures in an era without the luxuries of double-glazed glass, central heating, and air conditioning. Though insulation is often a factor in choosing a window treatment, ventilation and controlling natural light are more common concerns, today.

Any room with an eastern orientation is subject to strong morning light, a consideration acutely important in a bedroom, for example. A room with windows facing west gets strong light in the afternoon; however, if you're don't ordinarily use the room at this time of day, you may not care.

North-facing rooms, because they receive no direct sunlight, get chilly, especially during the winter. This makes a good case for insulated window treatments. Spaces with a southern

easily, is the solution. But don't ignore the way your window treatment looks from the outside. Choose a style that suits the building style of your home.

Four: **Observe the architecture.** The window treatment you choose is the bridge from wall to window. What you select should blend harmoniously with the room's design.

If there is a flaw in the design of the space, you can sometimes compensate for it with window decor. A treatment can add character that may be lacking or camouflage problems with scale and proportion.

Smart Tip

Always consider the way a window opens and closes before choosing a window treatment. Double-hung windows pose the fewest problems. However, casement windows and French doors that swing into a room require a design that will not obstruct their paths of operation.

Adjustable fabric-lined shades are practical in a nursery, left, that receives too much afternoon light when baby is napping.

Lightweight panels, below, loosely pulled back, hang from rings that move easily on the rod, allowing the French door to open without interference.

exposure receive the most natural light; during the summer months or in a warm climate, these rooms can get too hot. The right window covering can abate some of the heat buildup. Think about when and where you're most likely to be affected by natural light and whether you need a means to control it.

The rays of the sun also affect furnishings, so when choosing your window treatment, keep this in mind, as well. Delicate fabrics, wallcoverings, even wood finishes can be harmed by continuous direct exposure to strong natural light. Translucent fabric panels, once called "glass curtains," are often combined with draperies to filter sunlight.

Curtains and Drapery. Loosely hung fabric or panels that are attached to the window frame or sash offer some control over both light and privacy. The level depends on how many layers are installed and whether or not the fabric is lined. Sheer fabrics allow the transmission of light and don't obscure the view to the outdoors. Sometimes curtains and drapery are not adjustable; they have to be installed with a rod system or rings that allow you to open or close the panels to efficiently control light and privacy.

Shades, Blinds, and Shutters. All three are fully adjustable and offer complete control. They can be installed alone or paired with curtains or drapery.

THE DECORATIVE ROLE OF WINDOW TREATMENTS

A new window treatment can pull together an entire room, often unifying a design of disparate parts. It can change the style or ambience from casual to formal or from sterile to romantic. Different colors or prints can transform a nursery into a older child's retreat. New curtains can punch up, tone down, or blend into a color scheme, adding pattern and texture. The next chapter, "What's Your Window Style?" offers ideas and advice.

Vibrant print valances enliven the breakfast nook above. Tabbed café panels can be arranged on the rod to let in air when the windows are open.

A fantastic view is allowed to become part of the room's design thanks to simple Roman shades, left, that fold up during the day and unfurl for privacy at night. Their simplicity complements the clean architectural lines.

Full formal window treatments are appropriate in the period dining room at right.

What's Your Window Style?

A window is tied to a room architecturally and visually through its style. The more common types of windows, such as double-hung and casement units, may act as plain backdrops for window dressings. But specialty windows are often associated with a particular architectural style. Compare a triangular window with a Palladian one, for instance. The geometric shape of a triangular window has a modern sensibility, whereas the classic Palladian-style window is considered traditional.

When choosing a treatment, it is not enough to only look at the type and style of the window. You should examine how the window relates to the space around it—its visual weight. Is it a new fixed window in a room with a vintage fireplace and classical moldings? A window can sometimes go against all of the other decorative cues in the room. By assessing its style, you can coordinate the window with the space's decor. Is it a horizontal picture window in a room with low ceilings? This is a problem of proportion. Understanding proportion—and other decorating basics such as scale, balance, line, harmony, and rhythm—will help you to choose a treatment that looks as good on the window as it does in the room. This chapter will give you all of the information you need to identify and assess your window's style.

A Palladian-style window—a three-part opening with an arched center unit—is given a grand treatment with a crown cornice and boldly striped curtains, making it the focal point of this bathroom.

*A **casement window**, which has a rectangular sash, is topped with a Roman shade and a scarf swag. Ribbons were entwined with the scarf to add an extra note of color to the arrangement.*

A jalousie window has horizontal slats or narrow strips of glass that are opened louver-like by a crank. A sliding window or glass door has top and bottom tracks on which the sash moves sideways.

You should also explore the various architectural styles of windows, which often influence your decor. A group of three windows with an arch over the center unit is the classical makeup of a Palladian window. Some variations have three arches (one large, two small) or one fanlight-style arch over the three windows. This classical window tends to visually dominate a room, so it is logical as a focal point.

A picture window is made up of one large fixed window flanked by two casement or double-hung units. As the name describes, a picture window is for framing dramatic views. Like a Palladian or a picture window, a bay window is also composed of three parts. The difference is that the windows are set at an angle to each other, creating an alcove or bay. A curved version of this window is called a bow window. A large bay with a window adds about 4 feet of extra space to a room where you can situate a chair or a small dining table.

Window Types

To start, you should learn the basic types of windows and how they function. A fixed window cannot be opened and is often used with an operable window. A double-hung window is the most common of the operable types; it has two sashes that move up and down, which means that only half of the window can be completely open at one time. A casement window is hinged vertically to swing in or out.

A clerestory window is made of a strip of small, horizontal panes set high on a wall, near the ceiling. This window is often used in spaces where you want natural light but need privacy.

There are also a variety of special small window shapes that are almost strictly decorative. These windows are used independently or in combination with the standard types. An elliptical or arched window is often placed above double-hung or fixed windows, but it can also be used alone in situations where a larger unit won't fit, such as in a dormer or a small bathroom. An oval (or cameo) window and a circular window are used in much the same way; both are sometimes located on narrow staircase landings to add light. For a more modern shape, a triangular window or a trapezoidal window is often paired with a large fixed window—a combination known as a cathedral window.

Assessing Your Windows

Now that you've established the type of window you have, begin by examining how it relates to other elements in the room. Check how the window and the treatment coordinate. Look at the space itself—is there a prominent architectural style to the room? Also consider the size of the window

*A **bay window** requires a special curved track for drapery. Here, a tapered valance covers the hardware.*

Double-hung windows feature curtains with an oversized heading.

and how it relates to the space. To get you started, here are some easy steps to follow.

One: ***Compare the style of your window with the treatment you're considering.*** What kind of architectural detail does the window have or lack that you can cover up or enhance? Always remember that decorating and architectural styles are linked; not necessarily in the strictest sense, but there should be a relationship between the two. Heavy brocade panels paired with formal swags will appear out of place in a country parlor. In the same way, ruffled calico curtains strike the wrong note in a room that is streamlined and contemporary.

Two: ***Consider the size of the window.*** Particularly in older homes, windows are often too small, even for modest-sized rooms. Sometimes that's just because glass was expensive, so the windows were kept small. But many older houses also had no central heating at the time they were built, so the architect or builder used the same solution to avoid problems with heat loss. As homes were heated more efficiently and technologically advanced glazes were developed, window sizes grew larger. If your windows are small, you can create a more harmonious balance between the window size and the room with the right treatment and installation. For a short window, install the rod above the trim or just below the ceiling line. Hang extra-long panels, and let them puddle.

On the window that isn't wide enough for the wall, extend the window treatment beyond the frame on each side of the opening.

Some windows have the opposite problem—they're so large that they overwhelm the entire space. In this case, you can tone down the scale by keeping the look simple. If a window is too tall, don't use long panels. Break up the length by dressing the top of the window with a valance or a swag that's different from the rest of the design. When windows in a room are different sizes, de-emphasize the difference with curtains that are all the same length. Don't pile on several layers, and avoid heavily patterned fabrics. (For more information on working with problem windows, see Chapter 11, "Problem Solving," page 132.)

Three: *Take note of how a window functions.* Does the window open inward or outward? Does it slide on a track? Where is the handle for the crank located? This small—and seemingly obvious—detail can limit your window-covering choices. For instance, shutters

Roman shades *installed at the top of the wall heighten the window drama, right.*

A short valance *allows this bay of windows to take center stage, below.*

may impede inward-opening windows. Billowing curtains may get caught in the tracks of sliding glass doors. The crank handle on jalousie windows may interfere with blinds or shades. Knowing these limitations and conditions can help you choose the most practical treatment.

Proportion

Dressing a window is not always as simple as hanging up attractive curtains. A window covering should be in proportion to the window and the room. If an element is not the

right size—let's say, it has a rosette that's too small or an overly long valance—it throws off the entire effect of the treatment. The small rosette will be distracting rather than impressive; the long valance will make the window look squat and will make the room seem smaller. To plan a well-balanced window covering, there are several fundamental principles relating to space that you should understand. These principles include scale, proportion, line, balance, harmony, and rhythm.

Scale and proportion work hand in hand. In decorating, *scale* simply refers to the size of something as it relates to the size of everything else, including people and the space itself. *Proportion* refers to the relationship of parts or objects to one another based on size—the size of the

Identical treatment of the picture window and adjacent sliding glass doors provides a cohesive look in this room, left.

A simple treatment doesn't obscure the architectural elegance of the window, right.

Unobtrusive panels that hang from attached loops on a wooden rod open and close easily, below.

window is in proportion to the size of the room, for example. Good scale is achieved when all of the parts are proportionately correct relative to each other, as well as to the whole. If you are mixing patterns in an arrangement, for instance, you might want to balance the curtain's large-scale motif with a medium-scale design for the lining and a small-scale one for a border.

Occasionally, a window treatment turns out to be too large or too small for its setting. Careful planning and a deliberate effort will help you to avoid this and to achieve good proportion in the window covering itself, as well as its completed effect in the room. One way to test your ideas is to make a measured drawing of the window. (For more information on measuring windows, see Chapter 12, "Make Your

Own Curtains," page 148.) Then you can take your time and experiment with different arrangements on paper until something looks right.

Next to consider is *line*. Simply put, line defines space. Two-dimensional space consists of flat surfaces, such as walls, floors, and windows, that are formed by intersecting lines. Adding depth, or volume, to a flat surface creates three-dimensional space. However, lines do more than define physical space; they also suggest various qualities:

Vertical lines imply strength, dignity, and formality. Imagine how impressive a pair of tall, narrow windows flanking a fireplace would look.

Horizontal lines, such as a row of clerestory windows or even a cornice across a picture window, on the other hand, convey relaxation and security.

Diagonal lines, such as a triangular or trapezoidal window, express motion, transition, and change.

Curved lines, like those of an arched window or the shape of a swag, denote softness and sensuality.

Windows and their coverings are a way to incorporate a variety of lines into a room's design. Most modern rooms are rectilinear. Window dressings can help relieve the repetition of squares and rectangles inherent in the architecture. Tieback draperies or fan shades can introduce a few curves and make the space more interesting.

Balance is another important concept to consider. It refers to the equilibrium among elements in the window treatment. With balance, the relationships between the parts of an arrangement seem natural

The curves in the swag valance play up the graceful shape of this arch-top window.

*A **harmonious balance** of pattern and color exists in this design, which combines a soft valance over pleated shades.*

and comfortable to the eye. For instance, two windows side by side on a wall with matching floor-length curtains will look appropriate in a room, whereas the same setting with a sill-length curtain on one window and a floor-length curtain on the other will seem awkward and out of balance. Balanced relationships between objects can be either symmetrical or asymmetrical. *Symmetry* is when an arrangement is exactly the same on both sides of an imagined or real centerline. A swag with two matching cascade jabots is a good example of a symmetrical design. *Asymmetry* is an arrangement with elements of different sizes. For an asymmetrical design, picture that same swag with one long, cascade jabot. Both symmetry and asymmetry are thoroughly discussed in Chapter 7, page 86.

The two other design principles that should be considered when selecting a window treatment are harmony and rhythm. *Harmony* is achieved in design when all the elements relate to one another. In other words, everything coordinates within one scheme or motif. Matching styles, colors, and patterns are good examples of harmony. *Rhythm* refers to repeated patterns, which add movement and interest. For example, the scallops on a valance can be echoed by fan-edge trimmings on the curtain panels. Keep in mind that harmony pulls a treatment together, while rhythm moves the eye around the arrangement. The key to creating good harmony and rhythm is balance. Always add at least one contrasting element to your design for interest.

Smart Tip

Although it is important to keep architectural features in mind when choosing a window treatment, you can mix some styles. Classical windows don't have to wear formal swags and jabots; for example, simple panels or fabrics will let the architecture take center stage. Similarly, formal treatments can enhance architecturally plain windows.

What's Your Decor?

Window dressings often establish the overall look of a room. A good general rule is to match the style of the window treatment with the style of the interior. If the space is traditional, the curtains should be equally classical in their construction and fabric. Modern rooms call for up-to-date treatments. But like all rules, this one can be broken—or at least bent. The trick is knowing when to follow the established parameters and when to play against type. For that, you should analyze the room before you choose your curtains, which is what this chapter discusses.

As you examine your space, you are going to take note of color, pattern, and texture. These are the most important elements used to coordinate window treatments with interiors. Color can make windows eye-catching focal points or soothing backgrounds, depending on the effect you wish to achieve. Pattern can affect a room spatially, making it seem smaller or larger, depending on the scale of the design. The most subtle of the three elements, texture adds depth to a setting by incorporating fabrics with matte, coarse, smooth, and glossy weaves. To pull all of these pieces together, you will need to make a designer's sample board. This is an efficient way to combine—and edit out—fabrics in different colors, patterns, and textures. Doing this will help you select window coverings that add to the cohesiveness of the room's design.

Country-style rooms often feature a mix of patterns. The fabric chosen for the shades is the right scale and color to blend with the other prints in the room.

Assessing Style Needs

What do you want to achieve with your window treatment? It can enhance a space's good qualities by framing a beautiful view or incorporating color, pattern, and texture into the room. It can enliven a nondescript interior, serve as a focal point, or visually improve the room's spatial relationship. A window treatment is also an important way to establish a style. The wrong window dressing can throw off the entire decorating scheme. For example, ruffled calico curtains would look odd in a modern chrome-and-leather setting. To help you make a decision about your window-treatment needs, follow these steps.

 SMART STEPS

One: *Take note of the room's function.* In the previous two chapters, you looked at the window's function in a room—in terms of light control and privacy as well as how its architectural style influences a space. Now look at the use of the room itself. It often dictates the type of window treatment that is needed. In a dining room—a space used mostly for entertaining—a window dressing may be chosen for its dramatic effect. A bedroom with a window facing the street may need a cover-up for privacy. To cut the glare on a desk, a study may require shades or shutters. The purpose of a room may limit your window-covering choices.

Two: *Establish the style of the room.* Is it traditional? Contemporary? Period? Eclectic? Country? Window treatments set the tone of a room, enhancing the ambiance. Most types of treatments conjure an image of a certain style. Puddled drapery with a cornice are usually considered traditional; vertical blinds in a textured finish are more contemporary. You can break the rules—but it takes design confidence. For instance, classic toile de Jouy curtains can be combined with rustic rattan blinds in the right setting. Window dressings in a contrasting style can be used to tone down the negative aspects of a room's design. Instead of cabbage rose curtains, a cellular shade may keep an English country sitting room from becoming too fussy. Velvet drapery can add warmth and texture to a contemporary living room, which vertical blinds can't. To develop a trained eye for creating unusual combinations, look at interiors in magazines and visit designer showhouses.

However, most arrangements can be successfully designed by complementing the existing decor. For a romantic bedroom, nothing beats billowing sheers or the soft silhouette

An urban living room with a touch of classicism, left, needed an equally sophisticated window dressings. An elegant swag reinforces the window's status as the focus of this room.

A rose print coordinates, right, a multilayered arrangement with the upholstered chair in an English country living room.

of a balloon shade. The crisp lines of miniblinds enhance the simplicity of a modern living room. Gingham café curtains bring to mind country-style kitchens.

Also consider the decorating and architectural style of your home when planning your arrangement. How will the curtains or shades that you choose fit into the grand scheme? Visualize how the house will look from room to room, indoors and out. Although the window dressings in different rooms don't have to match, they should coordinate—particularly if you can see one space from another. Picture a hall that leads into a living room. The swags in the hall can be light green, picking up an accent color from the living-room curtain's floral print, for example. In this case, each space has its own style of treatment, but they are unified by a coordinating color.

Drapery in a cream color that matches the walls is a low-key choice for this comfortable and soothing bedroom.

Three: **Turn the window into a focal point, or make it blend with the decor.** A window that takes center stage in the room's design should be dramatic. Strong patterns or vibrant colors are both ways to grab attention, especially if the treatment itself is fairly plain. Elaborate layers of drapery with toppers, such as swags, valances, and cornices, steal the spotlight, too. Embellishments can do the trick—think trimmings, tassels, and rosettes. A word of caution, however: When making a focal point out of an arrangement, don't let it overpower the room.

Windows that blend into a room's design create a serene ambiance. To create a low-key background, choose fabrics or colors that exactly match the walls. Neutral hues and pastels are equally soothing. Sheers add a softness and delicacy that is never intrusive.

A small-scale pattern of stars makes this small dining room seem more spacious because it visually recedes.

Color

You can use warm colors and cool colors effectively to manipulate the way a window treatment is perceived. Because warm colors appear to advance, windows swathed in sunny hues seem closer together, making a room feel intimate. Conversely, cool tones and neutrals appear to recede and can be used to open up a smaller space. However, these color tricks can be employed more subtly. The less-intense version of a color will generally reduce its apparent tendency to advance or recede. Generally speaking, two contrasting colors, such as blue and orange, have the same impact as one dark color, reducing perceived space. Monochromatic schemes enlarge space, while neutrals of similar value make window treatments retreat. Keep these effects in mind when choosing a fabric color.

Pattern

Fabric is one of the most popular ways to add pattern to a room. Because pattern is largely a vehicle for color, the same rules that guide the selection of color effectively narrow the field when it comes to selecting a pattern or complement of patterns. The designer's old friend, scale, from Chapter 2, page 22, is the other important consideration when picking and mixing patterns.

A large-scale pattern is like a warm color in that it appears to come toward you. It can create a lively and stimulating atmosphere and generally make a large space seem cozier. In a small space, handle a large-scale pattern with care, or it can overpower the room. That doesn't mean rule it out completely, but perhaps use it sparingly. A small-scale pattern

Geometric patterns, such as the check and stripe curtains on these floor-to-ceiling French doors, are easy to mix and match.

Smart Tip

A trick for mixing patterns is to provide links of scale, motif, and color. The regularity of checks, stripes, textural looks, and geometrics, particularly if small-scale and low-contrast, tends to make them easy-to-mix "neutral" patterns. A small floral can play off a thin ticking stripe, while a cabbage-rose chintz may require a bolder stripe as a same-scale foil. Use the same or similar patterns in varying sizes, or develop a them by focusing on florals, geometric, or ethnic prints.

The matte surface of wool curtains makes this large room seem cozy and complements its rustic country charm.

appears to recede, making a small space seem larger. In a large room, the effect of a small pattern can be bland. From a distance it may read as a single color. If you're using a small-scale pattern on window treatments in a large space, pick one with vibrant colors.

Texture

Window treatments are a natural outlet for texture. Fabric choices for draperies and curtains, as well as the fabrics and other materials available for blinds and shades, are enormous and varied. Texture can be enhanced by the way fabric is hung. Pleating, for example, creates a play of light and shadow that looks three dimensional. You can combine layers of fabric and blinds to show off different textures.

Texture doesn't have the obvious impact on a window treatment that color and pattern wield. But how a material feels, as well as how it looks, does influence an arrangement's

design. Incorporating a variety of textures in a room adds to its richness in a way that's most comparable to the subtle inclusion of the line varieties discussed in Chapter 2, page 27. A mixture of textures plays upon the senses and adds another layer of complexity and sophistication to a design scheme. As with every aspect of decorating, mixing textures involves a balancing act. To give a room a distinctive character, you might let one texture predominate the room, but the right contrast can make the scheme intriguing.

FABRICS AND TEXTURES

The easiest way to incorporate texture into a design is with fabric. Brocades and damasks, moirés and chenilles, tweeds and chintzes—all conjure up different looks and sensations. Coarse and matte surfaces, such as tweed, wool, tapestry, and velvet, absorb light and sound. Glossy and smooth surfaces, which range from silk and satin to chintz and taffeta, reflect light.

Texture affects a room spatially. Coarse or matte fabrics on the window will make a room seem smaller and cozier. A living room of only glossy surfaces can appear impersonal and too expansive without tapestry draperies to make the space more snug and to add textural contrast. Smooth and shiny fabrics do the reverse—they make a room look larger and brighter. A study that feels stuffy, for instance, may benefit from pale-colored silk curtains. Light reflected off the fabric will make the space seem more open.

Keep in mind that texture can either soften or enhance a pattern. For instance, patterns are crisp on glazed chintz but are blurred on terry cloth. A coarsely textured surface tones down the intensity of a color, and gives the color subtle variations. High-gloss surfaces increase the intensity of a color. Think of how the gray color of a tweed jacket looks "heathered" and muted. On a silk shirt, however, the same gray color would look shimmery and more intense—a completely different effect. Because the fabric's weave affects the color, always test a sample of the material in the room.

Pulling It All Together

You've analyzed your room's decor, and you've established whether you want the window treatment to be a focal point. Now you need to choose a color scheme as well as mix and match fabric patterns. How do you find the best shade and pick the right pattern? Create a sample board.

One way designers analyze the colors, patterns, and textures for a window treatment is to put together a sample board. The white, foam-cored presentation board sold in art-supply stores, measuring at least $8^{1}/_{2}$ x 11 inches, is ideal for this purpose. Attach to the board with rubber cement (or tack to it with removable sticky material) any swatches of fabric, linings, and trimmings you're considering. (If you are decorating the entire room as well as choosing treatments, it is a good idea to include paint color chips, wallpaper samples, and fabric swatches for the furnishings so that everything can be compared together.) Keep swatches and other items in the same proportion on the board as they would be on the window. For example, a fabric sample that you're considering for the curtain panels will be large, whereas the lining in an accent color for a swag will take up far less space. Add and remove things as you experiment with different looks, and be certain to look at the board in the room for which it's created at different times of the day under both natural and artificial light.

To find the right match, a sample board was used to compare the swag's fabric with the wallpaper. The samples were analyzed in terms of color, pattern, and scale.

Lifestyle & Budget

Once you've decided it's time to put something on the windows, your first impulse may be to start collecting fabric samples and design ideas. Stop! Before you can choose a fabric or a window treatment, you need to determine what styles and components are compatible with your lifestyle and your budget. For example, goblet-pleat drapery made of white slubbed silk may be an elegant choice in a living room, but not for one in a home where a crayon-wielding toddler dwells. And tied shades, heavy drawback drapery, and other treatments that require daily adjustments are not practical or convenient choices if arthritic hands have to do the tying and pulling.

Budget concerns are twofold: How much *can* you spend? And how much *should* you spend? Curtains for a rented apartment generally call for less of an investment than drapery for a long-term family home, as do window treatments for a beach house, which may not be useful once the season is over.

How much you want to spend also determines whether to order custom window treatments, buy ready-made versions, or make them yourself. The first option typically includes professional installation. Complex designs often require special skills because the window treatments are actually constructed on the window itself. Ready-made window treatments are offered in a variety of sizes to fit standard windows. The style of home-sewn curtains depends

Custom shades were chosen for the large window to make an elegant statement because this living room is frequently used for entertaining.

Assess what type of interior you prefer. *A new apartment dweller softened the look of standard horizontal blinds that were already in place with pleated valances and puddled curtains in a romantic flower-covered print.*

on your level of skill. There are a number of attractive designs that beginners can tackle. (For more information about making basic curtains, see Chapter 12, page 146.) Researching the costs as you narrow down your options will help you make realistic, budget-wise decisions.

Lifestyle

In the previous chapter, you analyzed the room's function, noting any special needs or unusual problems that you have to address. Now you must examine your family's lifestyle. How you live influences all of your decorating decisions, and window treatments are no exception. What follows is a list

of questions to help you identify these lifestyle issues. As you review these questions, don't just make mental notes of the answers. Write them down. That way, you can refer to your responses on a regular basis. This will help you stay on track all through the process.

Personal Preference. What type of interior do you prefer? Window treatments can enhance—or even change—the overall atmosphere of a room. For example, after a long day at the office, you may want to relax in a soothing interior. Soft colors set the mood. Add curtains with a blackout lining, and you can darken a bedroom at will. Do you need a more stimulating space? Fabrics in cheerful colors or sheers that let in filtered light may do the trick. Do you like the look of a window dressed in several layers, such as a swag and jabot valance over drapery and undercurtains? Or do you prefer just one or two elements to achieve the desired effect?

Location. Start by asking yourself how long you will be staying in this space. Is it a permanent family home? Are you renting? Do you have a long-term or a short-term lease? Is this a second home, used only during specific seasons?

Seasonal spaces have their own special considerations. Window treatments may need to be dirt-resistant because the house will be shut up for part of the year. They may also need to be particularly durable if many different people will be renting the house.

Where you live can be as important a consideration as how you live. For a home in the city, privacy may be a greater

A seasonal home by the ocean calls for easy-care treatments like durable woven blinds and washable gathered curtains.

Privacy is a key issue for most homeowners. This room faces the backyard— as well as a neighbor's house. The vertical blinds are easily closed for seclusion.

issue than for a home in a suburban or rural area. Even where privacy is not a factor, relatively bare windows may make some family members uncomfortable. At night, the blackness of an uncovered window can have a chilling effect, particularly for those who grew up in homes where the curtains were always drawn snug at night.

External Appearances. Does your house have a particular architectural style that is more compatible with certain types of window treatments? Because you must consider how a treatment looks from the outside of the home, this can greatly influence your decision. For example, vertical blinds may not be appropriate for a traditional-style or historic house, yet may go seamlessly with a modern home. Exterior symmetry also may be important, particularly on

the windows at the front of the house. Check out the curb-side view. Treating the front windows in dramatically different styles may create a jarring effect.

Family Members. The number of people in a household is another point to consider. Are you single? Newlyweds? A retired couple? A family? If you have a family, how old are the children? Are there other dependents in the house, such as an elderly parent?

Single people and couples tend to have more choices and fewer restrictions. They don't have to take into account the tastes and habits of others in the household. Plus, there is less wear and tear on all of the furnishings, including window treatments. However, if young grandchildren are

In this child's room, a parade of pastel birds marches across a Roman shade. The raised shade stays neatly out of the way, leaving nothing to trip on; the looped cords are cut for safety.

How do your windows look from outside of your home? These white shutters create a unified appearance when viewed from the street.

frequent visitors, toddler-friendly window treatments—ones without dangling cords and puddled draperies—may be in order.

Families with young children should be realistic about their choices. Custom-made drapery in an expensive fabric may not last long after a few encounters with jam-covered hands. Attractive, washable cotton curtains, shutters with a beautiful valance, or swags with sill-length jabots may be better options. The choices expand when your children are older. Remember, however, that the rules that apply in your home may not be the same ones your kids' friends live with. Playing hide-and-go-seek behind the curtains can happen as quickly as your back is turned.

If you are caring for someone who is elderly or who has a disability, think about the weight of your window treatment and the ease of operation before you make a decision. Adaptations are available to make some window treatments simpler to operate. For example, push-button mechanisms can be installed to raise and lower Roman shades or to draw heavy drapery closed. Blinds with continuous-loop cords are easier to adjust than those with pull cords.

Pets can influence your choice of treatment, too. If your dog likes to curl up in cozy places, puddled curtains that billow onto the floor are not a good idea. If your cat is indiscriminate about where he sharpens his claws, choose a style that will be out of his reach, such as shutters or sill-length curtains. And even well-behaved pets may shed. A black

Smart Tip

It's generally a good idea to delay any final decisions about window treatments until you have determined your wall finishes, floor coverings, and overall color scheme. This way, your room's personality will be fully developed and the treatment you choose will complement the entire room. Rods, finials, and the like can be viewed as accessories, rather than hardware, that reflect the essence of the room. In addition, if you are considering a simple treatment, or relatively uncovered windows, this will give you the luxury of time to decide whether you are comfortable with the look.

Labrador retriever brushing past floor-length curtains in yellow gingham can be a hair-raising event that calls for daily vacuuming. Shorter curtains or pet-coordinated colors may save you from extra work.

Maintenance. Don't overlook maintenance. If a treatment requires frequent or expensive cleaning, consider whether it is right for you. For instance, if you travel often, you may not have the time to maintain formal drapery. The same is true if you have a house full of children—you don't need another task added to your list. Low-maintenance window treatments, such as miniblinds and a valance, may require less time and expense. This is not to say that formal treatments can't be low-maintenance—a simple valance with a pair of stationary panels may only need regular vacuuming to keep its good looks. But a multilayered window

Factor cleaning expenses into your budget because some treatments are more costly to maintain. A pleated-and-gathered valance may require professional dismantling, dry cleaning, and re-hanging every few years.

confection of double swags with cascade tails, rosettes, trimmed curtains, and sheers will take more attention. When heavy cleaning becomes necessary, you will probably have to call in a professional to dismantle the window covering, dry clean it, and re-hang it. If you entertain frequently, however, such treatments have unparalleled decorative impact that may be worth the extra upkeep.

Now take a look at the existing window treatments (if you have them). What's in place now may be a cue to the style and function of the new drapery. Assess both the good and bad points of the existing treatments. What do you like about them? Are there any problems? What should the new treatments do that these don't?

Assessing Your Budget

Figuring out a budget involves more than just finding out the price of a window treatment that you like. You must weigh the cost against the amount of money you have to spend, and how much it will cost you to maintain it. You also have to factor in how long you expect the treatment to last. In a rental apartment, you might want something that lasts only until you move. Or you may want to choose a look that is flexible enough to take with you when you leave. If you own your home, you may intend to renovate in a few years. If so, think about your plans for the rooms where these window treatments will reside. If you're a retired couple and plan to make this your last home, you may decide to pull out all the stops and go for something you've always wanted.

How a room is used may also influence your budget decisions. For example, if you entertain frequently, particularly for business purposes, then you may want to allocate a larger part of your budget to window treatments in the "public" rooms. If you are planning curtains for a baby's room, remember that what is cute for your infant now may not be appropriate when the child is nine or ten.

SMART STEPS

One: ***Become familiar with the costs of materials and services.*** Start by visiting showrooms, custom window-treatment shops, and home centers. Also call for catalogs with ready-made examples. Compare the prices. Evaluate everything, including the fabric, the lining, and the interlining, so you are comparing apples to apples. Don't forget the details: Take a look at hardware, such as holdbacks, poles, and finials, as well as tiebacks, tassels, and trimmings. If you are considering a custom treatment, talk to a design firm and find out about the fees for its services as well as the cost of installation. Because you haven't made any final deci-sions about the style, keep in mind that the prices you are gathering are only rough estimates. The purpose is to educate yourself about the cost of the various components so that you will be able to make realistic choices that are within your budget. If the costs seem too high, you might want to begin to explore some alternative routes, such as watching for sales or shopping the discount stores. If you are handy with a sewing machine, research some styles that are easy to make. Check out the pattern catalogs for some useful ideas. If you are considering the make-it-yourself alternative, be realis-tic about your capabilities. And remember to factor in your time as part of the cost.

Cost-conscious yet attractive, the ready-made floral valance and shirred curtain are good choices for this guest bathroom.

To fit this wide window, a custom-made treatment was designed. This one features puddled curtains and triple swags with jabots and golden-colored bullion fringe.

Two: **Choose a window treatment.** Now that you are familiar with pricing, you can hone in on the window treatment that suits your style and pocketbook. Review all of the stylistic possibilities. For a thorough guide to the choices, use Chapters 5, 6, and 7, which completely cover draperies and curtains; shades, blinds, and shutters; and cornices, valances, and swags. Now is also the time to decide what *type* of window treatment you plan to install: custom (through an interior designer), ready-made or semi-custom (through a retailer), or home sewn. If you don't want to go the custom-made route but are unsure about the style and color, look for an interior designer who will work with you on a consultant basis. For an hourly fee, he or she can help you narrow down the styles, fabrics, and colors that will best suit your needs and your decor.

Planning a Window Treatment in Stages

Stage One
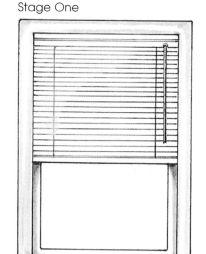

Stage Two
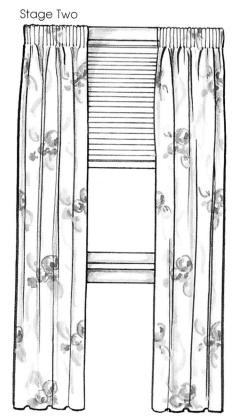

Stage Three

If you're on a budget, decorate your window in stages. Stage One is a covering for privacy, such as blinds. Stage Two can be a layer of drapery panels and a traverse rod. Stage Three adds details, such as a shaped cornice and silk tiebacks with tassels.

Three: ***Calculate the costs.*** Add up the price of the materials (face fabric, lining, and interlining, if any), trimmings, hardware, rods, and labor. As a safety net, add 15 to 20 percent to the total to account for any hidden costs. This will give you a general idea of the expense. If the final figure is beyond your means, you have two options. First, because this is the planning stage, you can still easily make some money-saving changes. Choose a less-expensive fabric, such as a cotton instead of linen, or simplify the design: Switch from labor-intensive goblet pleats to a gathered heading or opt not to use an interlining. However, you may not want to comprise on the design. If so, try the second approach, which involves doing the window treatments in stages. For example, a multilayered design may have a miniblinds, lined drapery, silk rope tiebacks with tassels, and a shaped cornice. Start by installing the most necessary element of the design—in this case, the miniblinds for light and privacy control. When you have the money, you can add the next layer, which consists of the drapery and the traverse rod. The last elements to be put into place are the luxurious extras—the cornice and the tasseled tiebacks.

Hiring A Professional

If you want professional help, be it from an interior designer or a custom workroom, do some homework. Don't just pick a name out of the phone book. Ask your friends and neighbors for referrals. Visit show houses; participate in house tours. These events, usually held in the spring to benefit local charities, offer you a chance to see the work of regional talent. Check out the home-fashion articles in local magazines and newspapers. Sometimes retail establishments can recommend professionals they've worked with in the past. If you have access to the internet, search for the Web sites of professional design organizations, which can often refer you to an interior designer in your area. Then, make an appointment to meet the designers or the custom workrooms that interest you. Look at their portfolios. Ask for at least three references—and be sure to call and check them. Lastly, contact the Better Business Bureau to see if any complaints have been lodged against the person or company you are thinking about hiring.

*An **interior designer's choice** of a cuffed curtain in a luxurious striped fabric hits the right note in this bedroom.*

Curtains & Draperies

I n the world of window treatments, curtains and draperies offer unparalleled versatility. These fabric-based coverings can be used to control the amount of natural light in a room, limit summer heat gain and winter heat loss, enhance or conceal a view, provide privacy, camouflage a room's bad points, create a needed focal point, or accentuate a decorating scheme. Seemingly endless variations in style, combined with almost limitless combinations of fabric, color, and trim, contribute to their popularity.

Throughout this book, the terms "draperies" and "curtains" are used interchangeably. But to some people, they have somewhat different meanings. *Draperies* are usually pleated, lined, and floor length, with a tailored, formal style. They are attached via hooks to a traverse rod; a cord mechanism is used to draw (close) them. *Curtains* are normally suspended from rods by rings, tabs, ties, or a rod-pocket casing; they are drawn by hand and have a more casual air.

When choosing curtains or draperies for your windows, you have to consider how far you will be able to retract the panels. *Stack-back* refers to how compactly curtains or draperies can be drawn back on a rod. When there is minimal wall space around a window or when you want to maximize a view, the depth of the stack-back is a concern.

Technically speaking, curtains are more casual in style. Instead of being hung on a rod, these scalloped curtains were tacked up, with rosettes covering the pins.

Curtain Basics

Curtains encompass three basic styles: panels, cafés, and tiers. Heading variations, including pocket casings, tabs, loops, ties, grommets, and pleats, can change the personality of each style. In addition, curtains can be lined, unlined, or—for extra body and insulation—interlined. All of these elements work together to influence the ultimate appearance of your window treatment.

TYPES OF CURTAINS

The basic *panel* is the most versatile and straight-forward type of window dressing. It can be any length and have any type of heading. It can be hung straight without any adornment or tied back in one of the various positions. It looks wonderful with all sorts of hardware, including traverse rods, decorative poles with finials, curtain rings, café clips, tiebacks, and holdbacks. This multipurpose treatment can be made in a variety of fabrics with trimmings—from fringe to gimp—to reflect any decor.

A *café curtain* covers the lower half of a window. A longer version goes approximately three-quarters up the window, leaving a small section at the top of the window exposed. Café curtains are usually hung from a pole by rings, clips, tabs, ties, or a rod-pocket heading. This type of casual treatment suits cottage-style interiors. Similar to café curtains, *tiered curtains* are a team of two half curtains covering the upper and lower sections of a window. They, too, have a homey, comfortable ambience and are hung on curtain rods.

Two floor-length curtain panels, with tabbed headings, frame the French doors in an elegant dining room. Curtain panels can feature any heading and can be made at any length.

CURTAIN LENGTHS

The curtain length influences the style of the treatment. A sill-length curtain has a casual air; drapery that falls to the floor connotes elegance. Curtain lengths also affect activity in the area near a window. Are the windows close to a breakfast table? If so, shorter curtains are less intrusive and leave clearance around the table. Is there a heat source underneath the window? Curtains should never touch or block a radiator, heat vent, or heating unit. Is the treatment hung on a glazed door? Make sure it doesn't block the opening.

Curtain lengths can camouflage window problems, too. Is the window awkwardly shaped? Or is there an architectural flaw that you would like to conceal? A floor-length treatment, hung above the window frame, can help disguise the problem. In some rooms, particularly bedrooms, windows may be different widths and lengths. If this is the case, plan the largest window treatment first. Dress the remaining windows in a scaled-down version of this treatment. For visual unity, install all the upper hardware at the same height.

In general, a window treatment looks best when it falls in line with the sill or floor. The most common lengths for drapery are sill, below sill, floor, and puddled. As the description implies, a *sill-length* curtain skims the windowsill. Favored for horizontal windows, it can start from the top of the window to the sill or, when café style, from the middle of the window to the sill. A curtain at this length is typically easy to operate, so it is a good choice for a window that will be opened and closed often.

The *below-sill length* falls at least 4 inches beneath the window frame so that it covers the apron, the horizontal board that runs under the sill.

Lace café curtains in this upstairs baby's bathroom are all that is needed on these casement windows because privacy isn't an issue and extra light is desirable.

Smart Tip

A breeze can stir up a floor-length curtain, leaving it in disarray. A *curtain weight* can minimize the problem, plus it helps drapery to hang more smoothly. There are two types of curtain weights: disk weights and fabric-covered weights. A disk weight is a small, round piece of lead that is inserted into the hem at each corner and each seam. To prevent it from rubbing and wearing out the fabric, insert it into a pocket made of lining fabric or muslin. A fabric-covered weight consists of links of metal encased in a fabric tube. This type, which comes in different sizes to correspond to the weight of the fabric, is attached along the hem.

If the curtain is too far below the sill, however, it looks awkward and unfinished. A sill-length panel, too, can be used for café or three-quarter curtains, and it can cover up an unattractive window frame. It generally looks best on picture windows and above window seats.

A *floor-length curtain* makes a strong visual statement. Make sure that the curtain is only $1/2$ inch above the floor because, like a hem that's too high on pants, floor-length treatments that fall short can suffer the "floods." (In humid areas, however, the curtain can be an inch off the floor to allow for the rise and fall of the fabric.) If you install layered drapery, the inner curtain can be $1/4$ to $1/2$ inch shorter than the outer curtain. To avoid seeing the back of the heading

*A **floor-length treatment,** left, looks appropriate in a formal dining room.*

***When puddling curtains,** below, increase the length of the fabric by at least 6 to 8 inches for the best results.*

Too Short

Too Long

Correct

from the outside, add 4 inches to the curtain's length so that it hangs above the window frame. This length works well with double-hung windows, bay windows, sliding glass doors, and tall, narrow openings, such as French doors.

Puddling is the term used for a floor-length curtain with an extra allowance of fabric that is arranged into a soft pouf (the puddle) on the floor. This is a dramatic length that falls 6 to 8 inches onto the floor. (For the correct length, see the

Sill-length tieback curtains in a yellow-and-blue Provençal print frame a window in a country-style kitchen.

illustrations on the opposite page.) Particularly appropriate for floor-to-ceiling windows, puddling has some drawbacks. A puddled curtain often needs adjustment, as it can be easily disarranged. Also, it isn't the right choice for high-traffic aisles or doorways, because the extra fabric can block the function of a door or cause someone to trip.

High Tie   Midway Ties   Center Tie

TIEBACK POSITIONS

How a curtain frames an opening is an important part of a window dressing's overall design. You can leave a curtain hanging unadorned, but by using a tieback, you can create a sculpted silhouette of fabric against a window. You can also control the amount of light that comes into the room and create a dramatic frame that enhances a view or covers an unsightly one.

Where you position the tieback affects the way a curtain hangs. The curtain can be caught back in a dramatic swoop of fabric, or it can be gently held open, revealing a colorful contrasting lining. The traditional tieback positions—high, midway, and low—are some of the most effective placements. Looping a tieback around or just below a pole, angled *high*, creates a short curve of fabric; don't use this arrangement where the curtain is moved often. A tieback positioned *midway* shouldn't fall exactly in the center; the best placement is slightly above or below the middle of the curtain. Two-thirds of the way down the curtain is the proper

place for a *low* tieback. When using this position, check that a tasseled tieback doesn't brush the floor, however.

A *center tie*—when one or two curtains are gathered at the middle so that they curve on both sides—can look impressive if it's on a bay or bow window. Use a rope tieback or, if the material is lightweight, literally knot the fabric. A *crisscross* arrangement requires two curtain rods and looks best with lightweight or sheer fabrics. When each panel is caught midway, the top halves overlap.

You don't have to limit yourself to one tieback per curtain. To create a *bishop's sleeve*, arrange two center ties at different points on a curtain (one high, one midway). Pull out the fabric above each tie to create a double tier of soft poufs. Try an *angled double tie* with a sheer undertreatment because the sinuous outline stands out against a gauzy backdrop. Slightly different from the bishop's sleeve, the two ties are arranged at the high and midway points on the panel so that the curtain swoops into graceful curves on only one side of the window.

Low Ties

Crisscrossed Ties

Angled Double Ties

How To Dress A Curtain

To make the folds fall evenly, train the curtains by tying them back for 48 hours or more. This is a process known as *dressing* the curtain and results in drapery that holds its shape and hangs well. To start, draw the drapery into the stack-back position. Fix the pleats and gaps in the heading until you are pleased with the arrangement. If the treatment is hanging below a curtain rod, position the gaps to fold toward the back; if the curtain hangs in front of the rod or pole, the gaps will fold forward. Smooth each pleat from the heading downward as far as possible. Then work from the bottom upward, gathering the pleats together. With a strip of fabric, make a loose tie just below the heading to hold the pleats in place. Make

another tie midway down the curtain, smoothing the pleats as you go. Follow with a tie by the hemline. The ties should be tight enough to hold the fabric but not so tight as to mark it. Next, steam the curtains gently, using a steam iron or a hand-held steamer. You may need a ladder to reach the top of the fabric, as well as a friend to hold the curtain while you fasten the ties. Leave the curtains undisturbed for a couple of days before removing the ties.

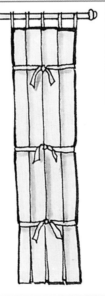

Putting It All Together

Whether you are choosing curtains for an entire house or just one room, the process is the same. You need to make three basic decisions about your treatment. Will it be formal or informal? Lined or unlined? What type of heading? Once these decisions are made, you can finalize a design that enhances your decor and meets your practical needs.

FORMAL VERSUS INFORMAL STYLE

A room's window treatments are influenced by a number of elements, including the function of the space, the architectural style of the house, and the decorating preferences of the homeowner. The result is that the same windows can

be treated quite differently. For example, picture a dining room with a bay window. That type of window is often given a multilayered, floor-length window dressing—in other words, a formal window treatment. But if you prefer a more casual style, you can choose the informal look of café curtains with sill-length, tied-back side panels.

A Full Formal Treatment. This often involves two or three layers. One layer, called the *casement curtain,* is installed inside the window's trim area. Typically it's a sheer, solid, or lace panel that lays straight or is gathered at the top. *Over-draperies,* often referred to simply as draperies, make up the second layer. Generally, they cover the window and the trim and, space permitting, extend beyond to the sides or the area above the window. The third, and optional, layer of a full formal window treatment is a *valance,* sometimes called a pelmet, which runs horizontally across the top of the window and covers the drapery or curtain heading. A hard valance, also called a *cornice* or a *lambrequin,* is usually made of wood and covered with fabric or upholstery. To some eyes, the window treatment is unfinished without this last element, but this is strictly a matter of taste. (See Chapter 7, "Cornices, Valances, and Swags," page 84.) Luxurious, heavy-weight fabrics, such as damasks, brocades, silks, tapestries, and velvets, enhance the sophistication of formal treatments. However, remember that these fabrics require professional cleaning every couple of years.

An Informal Treatment. This may consist of one or two layers or nothing at all. If location and privacy

Formal trimmings, such as the silk rosettes and black bullion fringe, add another layer to this arrangement.

considerations permit, a beautiful window looks attractive without a dressing—especially when there's also something pleasant to see outside. Sometimes simple casement curtains look attractive in casual rooms. If only the lower half of the window needs covering, café curtains offer privacy without blocking light. Fabrics that lend themselves to an informal look include all cottons, such as chintz, ticking, toile de Jouy, linen, gingham, and muslin. Unlike the fabric for formal draperies, most of these are washable.

LINING

The style of curtains—formal or informal—often dictates whether the treatment will be lined. Other considerations include how much natural light you want in a room and how long you expect the arrangement to last.

Unlined Curtains. An *unlined* curtain diffuses daylight, but it does not exclude it. It is the simplest form of window dressing, and it is effective on its own or as an undertreatment. Because an unlined treatment lacks the extra thickness of a lining, it stacks back tightly. Choose a fabric with no right or wrong side so that it looks equally attractive from both the outside and inside of the window. Voile, lace, muslin, and sheers made of cotton or silk organza are the classic fabric choices for unlined treatments. Textured fabrics with open weaves are also suitable.

An unlined curtain filters light beautifully and provides a hazy screen from prying eyes. However, because it offers little privacy in the evening when lamps are turned on, consider pairing sheers with shades or blinds. (See Chapter 6, "Shades, Blinds, and Shutters," on page 66.) Sunlight damage is

Lined, informal curtains, attached to curtain rings by green-striped ties, blend effortlessly with the white woodwork and pale green walls of this charming country bedroom.

another drawback to unlined curtains. Without a protective lining, the fabric deteriorates quickly.

Lined Curtains. A *lined* curtain has body, improving its appearance by creating softer, deeper folds. A lining blocks sunlight, protecting the curtain fabric and other elements in the room from fading, particularly where there is western or southern exposure. Sunlight also adds a yellow tint to unlined fabric that may throw off your room's color scheme.

A lining preserves the true color of the face fabric. Linings increase privacy, reduce outside noise, and block drafts and dust. Check for linings treated to resist rot and sun damage. Once a lining has deteriorated, the curtain can be relined or hung without the lining. To achieve the best protection possible, buy the best quality lining fabric you can afford.

If you line one curtain in a room, do the same to the rest so that the color and drape of the curtains match. Typically, lining fabric comes in white or off-white. Although colored linings are available, be aware that light shining through a lining affects the hue of a lightweight curtain fabric. Get samples of your intended lining and curtain fabric, and then test them together at the window for color change.

Interlinings. If you are set on having a colored lining, consider adding an *interlining,* which is a soft, blanket-like layer of material that is sandwiched between the lining and the curtain fabric. Like a lining, it increases the insulation and light-blocking qualities of the drapery, as well as extending the life of the curtains. It also gives a professional finish to pleats by improving the drape of the fabric.

A lining is usually sewn on, but it can also be attached with special double tape or pinned on with button-holes that slip over drapery hooks. The latter allows the lining and face fabric to be cleaned separately.

If you need a dark bedroom during the daytime because you work nights, try a *blackout lining,* which almost completely blocks sunlight. Other specialty linings include insulating and reflective types. These types of linings can be sewn on, but they can also be hung on a separate rod and drawn closed only when needed.

Diaphanous sheers, best left unlined, soften the outline of floor-to-ceiling windows without blocking any sunlight. If privacy is needed, the sheers can be paired with shades or blinds.

Interlining

An interlining, like the one shown at left, prevents the check lining from showing through the floral face fabric of this tent-inspired window dressing, above. The plaid ribbon, used as a border, is a transitional element between the two patterns.

CURTAIN HEADINGS

The *heading* is the top of the curtain. It's the opposite of the bottom hem. How it is constructed helps establish the type of the curtain. Headings encompass a variety of styles—from a simple casing, or fabric pocket, that holds a drapery rod to complex folds that are intricately pleated to create a decorative effect. Some headings, such as tied or tabbed styles, tend to be casual, while others, such as goblet and cartridge pleats, are formal. On the following pages, many different types of headings are discussed and illustrated.

Rod-Pocket & Gathered Headings

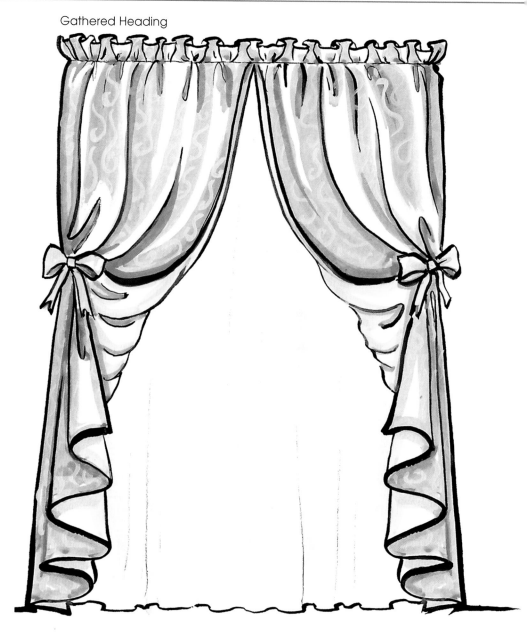

Gathered Heading

A simple design is often the most effective one, which is true of rod-pocket and gathered headings. A *rod-pocket heading*, also known as a slot heading, is a casing (a tunnel-like pocket) created by turning the top of the curtain fabric down twice and then stitching it along the bottom fold. The rod is then slipped into the casing, and the curtain is gathered.

A rod-pocket heading can be plain, which means it lays flush against the rod, or it can have a ruffle. This ruffle is typically 2 to 4 inches deep.

Because it is difficult to reposition the fabric on the rod, choose a rod-pocket heading in situations where the curtain remains stationary. This unpretentious heading pairs well with a short, light-weight style. However, a curtain with a rod-pocket heading can also be lined and extended to the floor.

Rod Sleeve. When a rod-pocket heading is used on large openings, such as a picture window or a sliding glass door, the curtains purposely remain at the sides of the opening, leaving the rod exposed. If you don't like this look, try unifying the treatment with a *rod sleeve*. Used in place of a valance, a rod sleeve is

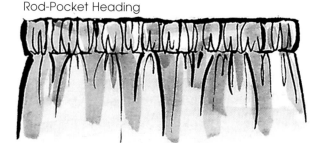

Rod-Pocket Heading

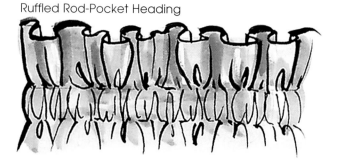

Ruffled Rod-Pocket Heading

a simple casing that is gathered over the rod to visually bridge the gap between the curtain panels. Match the style and fabric of the sleeve to the heading. If the heading has a ruffle, try a sleeve with a double ruffle—one above and one below the casing—to add detail.

GATHERED HEADINGS

A *gathered heading* is a soft, 2- to 4-inch ruffle created by draw-cord tape, a strip of material with strings that are pulled to create the gathers. It hangs from curtain rings or hooks. An oversized ruffle, one that is 6 inches or more, creates a *cuff*—a valance-like edging—on a gathered heading. (A cuff can also be a separate piece of fabric attached to the top of the curtain panel.)

Bunched Heading. A rod-pocket or a gathered heading with an oversized ruffle can be converted into a *bunched heading.* This is achieved by pulling the ruffle's layers apart so that it is puffed up. (To add extra body, insert a piece of interlining into the heading.) The ruffle of a bunched heading can also be secured with stitches to create a scrunched effect. The larger the ruffle, the more pronounced this effect will be.

A gathered heading is compatible with most styles of curtains—long or short, lined or unlined. Because it is hung from curtain rings or hooks, it is much easier to adjust than a rod-pocket heading. When a gathered heading is hung from curtain rings, it exposes a section of curtain rod, so pair it with hardware that has pizzazz. However, when it is hung from hooks, the traverse rod usually won't be visible.

*This **bunched heading** was scrunched up and secured with stitches. Note how the window decor in this eclectic living room mixes styles: The bunched heading shows off the luxurious silk fabric and a plain heading suits the gauzy sheer curtain.*

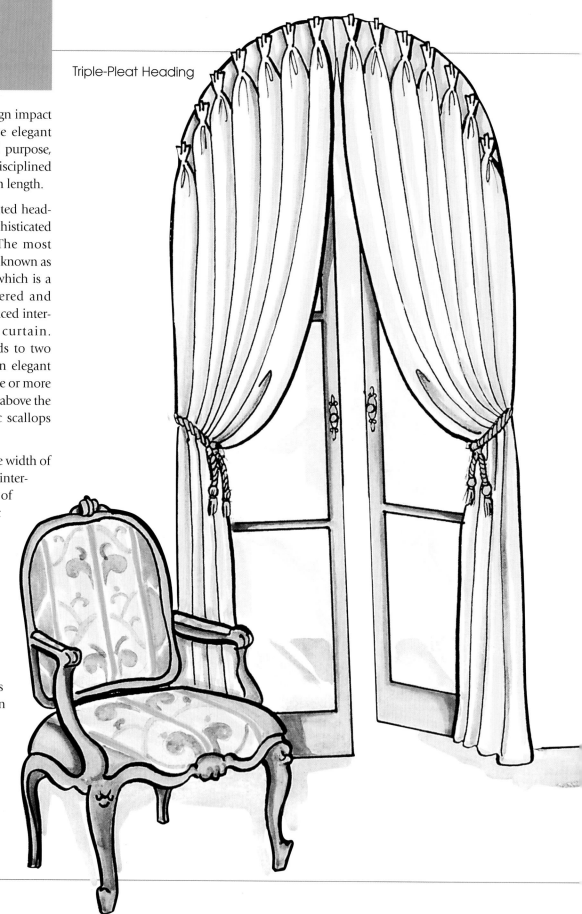

Triple-Pleat Heading

Pleats offer the greatest design impact of all the headings. These elegant arrangements have a practical purpose, too: They create supple yet disciplined folds of fabric down the curtain length.

Pleat Types. The styles for pleated headings range from the subtly sophisticated to the impressively grand. The most common is the *triple pleat*, also known as the French or pinched pleat, which is a trio of folds pinched (gathered and secured) together at evenly spaced intervals along the top of the curtain. Reducing the number of folds to two creates a *butterfly pleat*. For an elegant look, a *fan pleat* is made of three or more gathered folds that rise slightly above the curtain rod so that the fabric scallops between the fans.

A *pencil pleat* is the approximate width of its namesake. It is part of an uninterrupted row of pleats. Because of the simplicity of this classic heading, use pencil pleats for draperies that are meant to blend with your room's decor rather than stand out; pencil pleats often top draperies that are tucked under valances or cornices. (See Chapter 7, "Cornices, Valances, and Swags," page 84.) By fastening pencil pleats into a latticework pattern, an elaborate *smocked heading* is created. A *box pleat* is folded so that two pleats meet, creating flat plains of fabric; although used more often for valances, box pleats can work well for draperies, particularly contemporary or tailored styles.

For a dramatic treatment, the fold of a *goblet pleat* is formed into a cup-like shape above a pinch. To emphasize the shapes, cording is often attached by the pinch, linking each goblet in what is called a *Flemish heading*. A *cartridge pleat* is a tubular-shaped fold without a pinched section. Both goblet and cartridge pleats are usually stuffed with a small piece of lining or batting to pad the shapes; a piece of fabric in a contrasting color can be added on top of the stuffing to emphasize the design.

Stiffeners & Tapes. To look its best, a pleated heading requires a backing made of a stiffener, such as buckram—a course cloth stiffened with glue—or a tape to keep the design in a neat formation. If the pleats are hand-folded, buckram is used to make the heading firm. Buckram comes in 4- to 6-inch widths, and it is attached by sewing or, if the fusible type, ironing.

Pleating tape, which is a strip of cotton or nylon with strings running through it, gathers the curtain fabric into the desired type of pleats when the strings are pulled. The tape ranges from 1 to 5

*A **fan heading** is suited to an arrangement where it won't be moved. Here, no hardware was used at all. The heading is tacked onto the window frame.*

inches wide and has pockets for inserting the drapery hooks. Like buckram, it can be sewn or fused to the back of the heading. Tapes provide good results if you are making pencil pleats, but more complex headings, such as box, triple, and goblet pleats, often turn out better when made by hand with a buckram backing.

Pleated curtains are often lined and interlined to add fullness. Because of the extra weight from the lining and interlining, make sure these draperies are securely hung from a stationary or a traverse rod; lightweight versions can be hung from curtain rings on a curtain rod.

Fan-Pleat Heading

Pencil-Pleat Heading

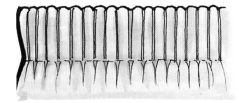

Smocked Heading

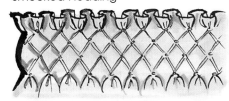

Box-Pleat Heading

Goblet-Pleat Heading

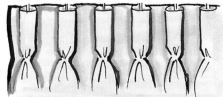

Cartridge-Pleat Heading

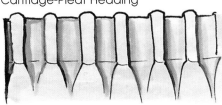

Tabbed & Tied Headings

The casual elegance of tabbed and tied headings has recently grown in popularity. A *tabbed heading* is a looped piece of fabric with an exposed end (the tab) that is often adorned with a button; the button can be functional or decorative. Akin to a tabbed heading, a *looped heading* is a band of material without a visible tab end; it can be made of fabric, ribbon, or rope. Sometimes the

For tabbed curtains, when working with a striped fabric, make sure to align the stripes on the tabs with the ones on the curtain panel. Buttons can be covered to match.

fabric between the loops is scalloped, an effect favored for café curtains. A *tied heading* consists of two fabric strips that are tied in a bow onto a curtain rod.

Tabs, loops, and ties are often highlighted by fabric that contrasts with the curtain material. Another decorative accent for these headings is a cuff.

Even with a lining, these headings take up little stack-back space. However, tabbed and looped headings can be hard to adjust, so use both in stationary arrangements. By fastening a tied heading to curtain rings instead of directly onto the rod, it will move back and forth more smoothly.

Tabbed Heading

Tied Heading

Looped Heading

Pierced & Plain Headings

Because pierced and plain headings hang from grommets or rings, they are relatively easy to move. A *pierced heading* is a series of either buttonholes or grommets (eyelets) that perforate the top of a curtain. The curtain rod is threaded through these openings. To vary this heading, short pieces of ribbon or cord can be pulled through each grommet and tied to the rod. A curtain with a pierced heading can be lined. To help hold the shape, use a strip of buckram to reinforce and support the heading area.

Before making a pierced heading, always check that the curtain rod fits through the grommet. If you can't find a rod that is narrow enough, consider using curtain wire, which is hung on brackets.

A *plain heading,* as the name implies, is simply hemmed without pleats or tape, and then attached to curtain rings or to café clips. A lining may be added, but the extra weight may be too much for café clips. Adorn a plain heading with cuffs, borders, or bows to add definition and form. Because the rod is so visible, choose eye-catching hardware. Buckram makes a plain heading lay flat; for a softer look, try interfacing, a pliable material often used in dressmaking.

Before making a pierced heading, check that the grommets fit on the rod. A buckram backing creates stiffer folds of fabric.

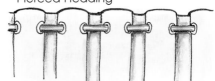

Pierced Heading

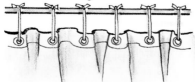

Pierced Heading with Cord Ties

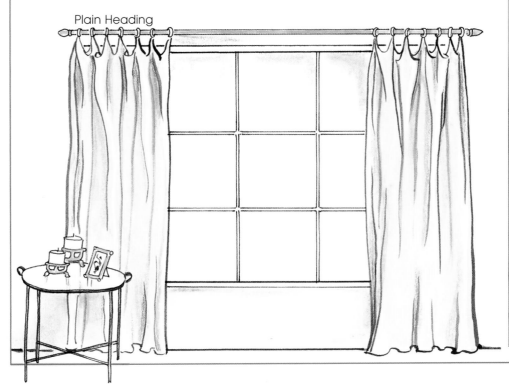

Plain Heading

Shades, Blinds, & Shutters

Shades, blinds, and shutters offer a variety of options for dressing the window and filtering the light. Some shades completely block the light when lowered, while others are designed to diffuse the sunlight that enters the room. And some shades can be raised to expose almost all of the window glass, while others can be only partially raised. Blinds, on the other hand, don't have to be raised to perform these same functions. Simply re-angling the slats does the trick. As a category, blinds impart a crisper, more tailored look to windows. Shutters, more than any other window treatment, bring an architectural element to the room. Other window treatments look like a fashion choice; shutters, once installed, appear to be an intrinsic part of the home's basic character, much like crown moldings and floorboards.

Any of these treatments can adorn a window as its single element, providing clean lines and a pared-down simplicity that goes with the modern aesthetic for interiors. But just as frequently, these treatments are one part of the total picture. Shades, blinds, and shutters can complement an existing window treatment in terms of fashion and supplement it in terms of function. Curtains, valances, cornices, swags and jabots, in all their many styles, add layers of decorating punch to these looks.

Bamboo shades, with their golden color and textured surface, complement the informality and warmth of this home office.

Shades

A shade is a window treatment that is raised and lowered by means of a spring mechanism or cording system. This simple definition covers a great range of styles, from flat shades to softly draped festoon shades. Today, window-shade choices go far beyond the basic vinyl roller shade and into a whole world of exciting fashion choices. But before you decide which shade will grace your window, it is important to analyze your needs and understand your options.

SMART STEPS

One: ***Consider light control and privacy.*** Are you looking for daytime control, nighttime control, or both? Do you want maximum light during the day but complete privacy at night? Will the shade have to accomplish these objectives alone, or are you pairing it with other elements that can help out? For example, you can combine a light-filtering shade that gives sun protection in the daytime with draperies that can be closed for privacy in the evening. Some roller shades and pleated shades can be installed bottom-up, covering the lower portion for all-day privacy while admitting light above.

If frequent adjustment is necessary, how easy is the operating mechanism? This may depend on the age and manual dexterity of the user. While adults find roller shades easy to adjust, small children often have problems.

Two: ***Decide how you want the treatment mounted.*** Shades can be mounted inside or outside the window frame. Your decision can be a purely aesthetic

Two shades are mounted on this bedroom window. The bottom cellular shade filters light while providing privacy. The Roman shade, which is raised into the cornice here, has a blackout lining for daytime sleeping.

Inside Mount

Outside Mount

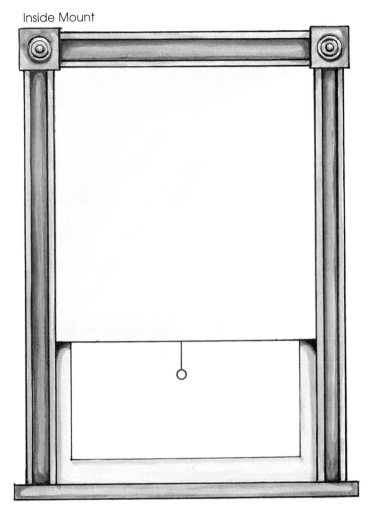

one, or it can have some practical reasons behind it. An *inside mount* is generally used if the shade will be paired with a top treatment, such as a valance or a swag, or with a treatment that would interfere with its operation, such as drawn curtains. It is also used if the window has a particularly handsome frame that you would like to show off or if there isn't enough room outside the window frame for the operating mechanism. From a design point of view, an inside mount permits the window frame to outline the treatment, giving it visual emphasis.

An *outside mount* is used if you want to conceal the window frame, camouflage the size of the the window, or simply leave a larger expanse of window treatment on view.

Three: ***Choose a shade style.*** There are many different styles of shades. Some have their own intrinsic decorative character, while others are more chameleon-like, depending on fabric and trimming. For example, cellular shades and pleated shades (page 71) have a contemporary appearance. For a softer appearance, they can be combined with another element, such as a valance. Because the fabric is gathered, balloon shades, cloud shades, and Austrian shades (pages 74-75) have a softer, dressmaker ambiance.

Roller shades, Roman shades, and cascade shades (pages 72-73) can easily change their personalities. When solids and geometrics are employed, they tend to have a more tailored air than when florals and laces are the chosen fabrics.

Scalloped & Curved Hems

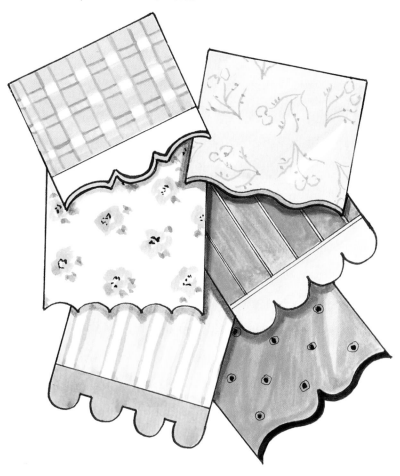

Four: **Consider a hem design.** Hems can be plain or intricate. But not all shades offer the same creative hemline opportunities. Pleated shades and cellular shades do not lend themselves to fancy hems.

Rollers shades, however, are the perfect canvas for a variety of hem treatments. Decoratively shaped options include scalloped, curved, geometric, and notched hems. Instead of a conventional shade pull, roller shades can have a double layer at the lower edge that is notched so that a rod can be inserted through the hemline, creating an openwork design with a stable base. These edge treatments can mirror a pattern or motif found elsewhere in the room.

Decorative trims, including fringe, cording, ruffles, lace edgings, ribbon, and rickrack, can dress up the hemline of shades with cording mechanisms, such as balloon shades, cloud shades, and Austrian shades. Shades that tie, such as roll-up shades, usually have a plain hem because an embellished one would interfere with the shade's operation.

You may already have set ideas about the kind of finishing detail you want, or you may put this decision on hold until you have further explored the attributes of each individual type of shade. If you need to learn more, the information about shades on the following pages will help you reach the right decision.

Geometric & Notched Hems

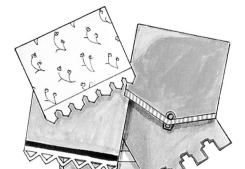

Rod & Notched Hems

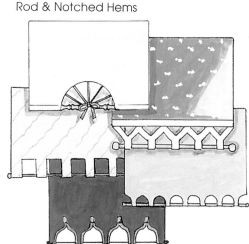

Fringed, Corded & Ruffled Hems

Pleated Shades

Pleated shades are a soft alternative to traditional blinds with the additional benefit of diffusing light. They come in many configurations, including ones for round, arched, and elliptical windows. Because one large shade is difficult to adjust, wide windows generally require two or more shades.

Special options include a double-cord control that allows you to move the shade in two directions—from the bottom up and from the top down (see below). Also, a track system with a split headrail makes it possible for two shades to operate on the same track. This feature is handy if you need two different types of shades, such as one for privacy or sun-filtering and one for color or style.

Basic Pleated Shade. A pleated shade is made of permanently folded paper or fabric. This type of shade stacks compactly—for instance, a 6-foot-long shade can pull back to under 3 inches. Pleats usually run as wide as 1 to $1\frac{5}{8}$ inches. Some fabric shades have a backing layer that offers high-energy efficiency, complete control of light, and privacy. Plus, they create a uniform appearance from outside the house.

Cellular Shades. A cellular shade is made of two or more layers of folded fabric, which create honeycomb-like "cells." (See right.) Cellular shades offer a number of benefits, ranging from UV protection to privacy control to insulative qualities. Stationary versions can be made for special window shapes, such as arches and ovals.

Cellular Shade

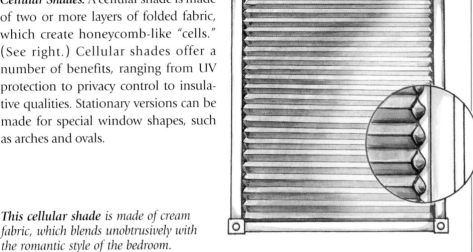

This cellular shade *is made of cream fabric, which blends unobtrusively with the romantic style of the bedroom.*

Pleated Shade

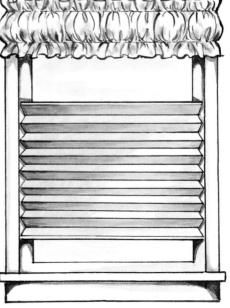

Basic and batten shades are those that, when lowered, present a smooth surface against the window. This category includes roller shades (firm shades that can be made from fabric or vinyl), roll-up shades, fan shades, cascade shades (soft, stationary shades that have a distinctive draped effect when they are raised), and Roman shades (which are relatively firm and usually made from fabric).

Roller Shade. This type of shade can be purely functional or highly decorative. It is particularly good for a small window where you want to take advantage of the light. Generally, a roller shade is operated by a spring mechanism that is activated by tugging at the lower edge. This

lower edge can be plain or embellished in any number of ways. A decorative pull (handle) can also be added to prevent wear on the lower edge of the shade.

The shade itself is made from vinyl or a tightly woven fabric. The fabric is either laminated (glued) to a backing or is treated with a stiffening agent to give it firmer body. You can purchase roller shades in a variety of colors (usually neutrals and pastels), textures, and finishes. You can also have shades custom-made to match or complement fabric used elsewhere in the room. And you can make your own shades, using your own fabric. Kits are available that contain a roller with a built-in winding mechanism, brackets, wood batten (bottom slat), and hardware. To stiffen the fabric, treat it first with a special liquid or spray stiffener, or apply an iron-on backing designed specifically for shades.

Fan Shade

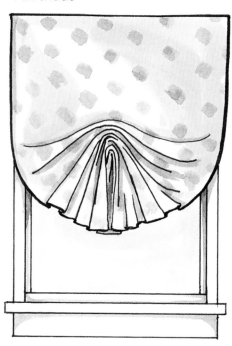

Roll-Up Shade

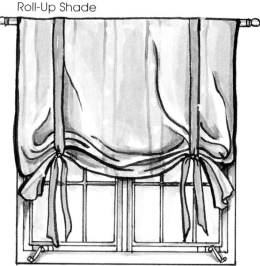

*For **an alternative** to a loosely hanging bottom edge (above), sew a dowel into the hem of a roll-up shade to keep it straight (left). Here, thick cording replaces the traditional fabric bow ties.*

*This **Roman shade** is made from a fabric with a clever teacup print, the pattern of which isn't obscured when raised.*

scooped shape. To stabilize the shade, a rod can be inserted along the lower edge, centered between the rings. Because this shade is usually unlined, choose a fabric without a right and wrong side.

Fan Shade. This type of stationary shade has a single set of rings and cords that raises the center of the shade. This causes the sides to swing down, creating fan-shaped folds. Two battens, inserted along the hemline and meeting at the center, stabilize the shape. It looks best in plain and small-patterned fabrics, and it has a more formal appearance than other fabric shades.

Roman Shade. Unlike roll-up and fan shades, Roman shade is a fabric shade that can be raised or lowered at will. When raised, it folds up evenly at regular intervals. These folds are created by a system of rings, cords, and precisely spaced horizontal battens. It is not hung on a rod. Instead, a Roman shade is mounted on a board that is attached inside the window frame or on the wall above the frame to let in full light.

This versatile treatment can be lined and insulated or made from a single layer of sheer fabric. A Roman shade can be designed so that it is smooth when lowered or has small, overlapping folds. A fold should never be more than 8 inches wide because the shade will not pull up evenly and the battens will bend. For wide windows, use multiple shades. Beware, too, of horizontal stripes and some large patterns; they may not align attractively when the shade is raised.

Roll-Up Shade. A roll-up shade, sometimes called a tied shade, is stationary. It is a good choice where there is an unattractive view or where it won't be adjusted often. If it hangs from a pole or a shelf mounted outside the window frame, there should be enough room on the wall on both sides of the window to install the brackets. Once the shade is hung, the bottom part is rolled up to the desired position and secured with ties. The shade can be designed so that the lower edge folds into a soft swag when tied or the lower edge can be reinforced with a batten. It needs a fabric that isn't too heavy but will stay in place, such as a silk taffeta. Strong, bold patterns work well on this particular type of shade. For visual punch, use contrasting ties.

Cascade Shade. This type of shade is similar to a roll-up shade, but it usually has two sets of rings and cords sewn in a vertical arrangement onto the back of the shade. When the cords are pulled up, the sides swing in, giving it a

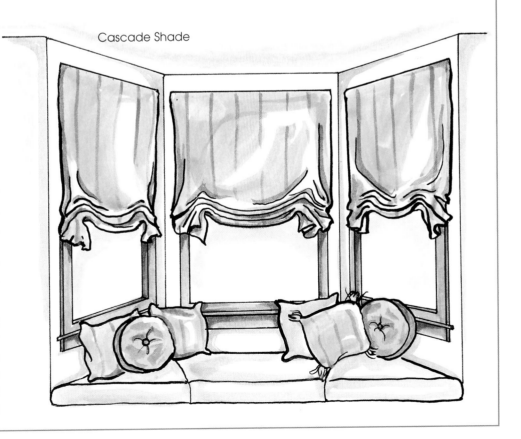

Cascade Shade

Festoon Shades

Festoon shades are gathered fabric shades that add softness and femininity to a room. They are designed to be raised or lowered by means of a ring and cord system that is attached to the back of the shade. When extended full length, festoons look like a gathered and scalloped curtain. When drawn up, they get fuller, with rounded, poufed-up edges.

The amount of fullness—or pouf—can be controlled by the placement of the cords and rings. Wide spaces between them means shallower scallops. Narrower spaces mean deeper scallops. It is not necessary for all the scallops to be the same width. For example, a festoon could have a wide scallop in the center and narrow ones at the ends.

Balloon Shade

Tailed Balloon Shade

Balloon Shade. A balloon shade is gathered in scallops across the width of the shade and is raised in soft folds by a cording system. Although it can be designed with one scoop, a balloon shade is typically three to four scallops wide and has an inverted pleat heading. The result is a slightly tailored shade with ruching that falls only along the scallops.

When lowered to floor or sill level, a balloon shade looks like a full-length curtain. However, if you prefer the scalloped shape, increase the length of the fabric so that the ruching remains even when the shade is completely lowered. To accent the shape of the hem, add ruffles or fringe. (Smaller details, such as cording, won't show up.) Another hem option is called *skirting.* Leaving off the

This sunny yellow cloud shade, with its cushiony fullness, is a pleasing contrast to the straight geometric lines of the bookcase in this child's room.

When an Austrian shade is lowered, the multiple folds are still visible down its length. Lightweight fabrics, such as this white sheer, shows off the exuberant folds to best effect.

bottom rings creates a flat panel, over which the scallops fall.

Choose fabrics in solid colors or simple patterns for balloon shades. Stripes, checks, plaids, miniprints, and small-scale florals work well, but bolder patterns may look excessive and may be distorted by the ruching.

Tailed Balloon Shade. By omitting the side cords on a balloon shade, a *tail* is created. Tails can be just a few inches long or dramatic drops that are double the width of the scallop. Long tails looks best with shades that are only one or two scallops wide. Shorter tails are better when there are multiple scoops. Ribbon or contrast binding along the lower edge or sides accentuates the shade's shape.

Cloud Shade. When a balloon shade has a gathered or pleated heading, such as a pencil pleat, it is often referred to as a *cloud shade*. A cloud shade has a scalloped hem and exuberant ruching, which results in a very feminine treatment. The lower edge is usually left plain or trimmed with a deep ruffle; a narrow trim would simply get lost in the billowy edge.

Austrian Shade. This shade first came into fashion during the eighteenth century. The full fabric length is at least double the drop of the shade. As a result, even when the shade is completely lowered, horizontal scallops remain. It is an opulent style of shade. Often made from a sheer or lacy fabric, it looks great alone or as an undercurtain for heavy draperies.

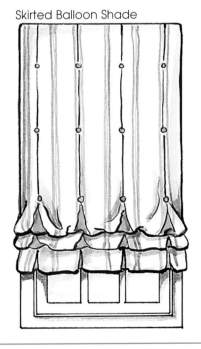

Skirted Balloon Shade

Cloud Shade

Blinds

Blinds encompass a group of hard window treatments composed of movable slats. Blinds can be raised and lowered; many versions can also be opened and closed to permit varying degrees of light to enter the room. They have a linear quality that is compatible with tailored and contemporary interiors. For a traditional decor, blinds are usually combined with curtains for a softening effect.

Woven together to make blinds, off-white (or other color) quills like the ones in these window are an attractive alternative to cane or wood. Plastic has the advantages of coming in a range of colors and exhibiting resistance to moisture.

MATERIALS

Slats are made from a variety of materials that are generally firm or rigid in nature. These slats are strung together so that they can be rolled up, usually on a spring mechanism, or pulled up with a cord.

Paper. Paper blinds are pleated so that the creases remain even when the blinds are down. They are easy to dust, inexpensive, and available in a wide range of colors. Optional metallic backing repels the sun in the summer.

Cane. Whole or split cane, such as bamboo or rattan, is used for blinds that roll up or fold into pleats. Small spaces between the slats let through some light, which makes blinds made from this material translucent from inside and outside the room.

Metal. Aluminum alloy is the traditional material for Venetian blinds, which have slats that are slightly curved. They come in a variety of widths, from $1/2$ to 2 inches wide, can be custom-fit for special-shaped windows, or cut to fit around air conditioners.

Wood. For Venetian blinds, these slats are 1 to 2 inches wide. Tapes or thin cords control the movement. Adjusting the angles of the slats controls the amount of light. The slats can be stained or painted. They offer a natural look, durability, and insulating properties. Woven cloth tapes are available with wood-slat blinds in coordinating or contrasting colors. Narrow strips of wood are also used for woven blinds.

Plastic or Vinyl. These 1-inch slats function the same as wood or aluminum versions but are less expensive. Aside from a range of colors, options include high-gloss and pearlized finishes.

Fabric. Stiffened, textured fabric is often used for vertical blinds. For specialty blinds, fabric slats form an interior layer that is sandwiched between two sheer facings. The sheer fabric softens the hard lines of traditional blinds. Plus, when open, it lets light filter into the room and provides some degree of privacy.

Woven Blinds

As a category, woven blinds tend to be informal in style and contribute to the casual, outdoor feeling of a room. They are good for family rooms, sun rooms, and porches, but they also show up in kitchens and bathrooms. Woven blinds comes in standard sizes and are composed of inexpensive materials, making them the most reasonably priced option when compared with other types of blinds.

To create these blinds, narrow horizontal slats are woven together using strips of cotton twine. Woven blinds may be mounted inside the window with screw-and-eye hangers. A pulley system pulls the blinds up. They can be fixed at any level by winding the cord around a cleat that is attached to the wall. Use them alone or with a top treatment.

Matchstick Blinds. This blind is made from very thin strips of natural fibers, usually cane or basswood. A matchstick blind can be stained, painted, or left natural. It filters the light during the day but, because there are spaces between the slats, it does not offer complete privacy during the day or night.

Plastic Blinds. Similar to a matchstick blind, this type is constructed from narrow plastic slats, called quills, with closely spaced strips of twine. It comes in white and a wide range of colors. Plastic blinds are somewhat less bulky than matchstick blinds.

Because a matchstick blind can be seen through when lowered, it provides only a slight screening. The woven rattan blinds in this comfortable sitting room act as a stylish backdrop in a location where privacy isn't an issue.

Matchstick Blind

Plastic Blind

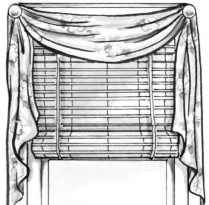

Horizontal & Vertical Blinds

Traditional slatted blinds come in a wide variety of materials and finishes. Used alone, they have a linear, almost industrial quality that works well in a contemporary setting. However, it is easy to warm up blinds by pairing them with curtains or any of the fabric top treatments.

Venetian Blind. Usually made from aluminum, this blind consists of a series of 1-, 2-, or 3-inch-wide horizontal slats held together by cords and twill tapes.

The slats can be raised, lowered, or angled to control light. It comes in many colors and finishes, including anti-static, metallic, pearl, suede, and a perforated finish that permits light to enter even when the blind is closed.

Wood-Slat Blind. A Venetian blind constructed from wood is called a wood-slat blind. The finish can be natural, stained, or painted. Because wood slats are thicker, wood blinds have a deeper stack than aluminum when pulled up. When down, this blind is reminiscent of shutters, particularly when the slats are in the closed position.

Wood-Slat Blind

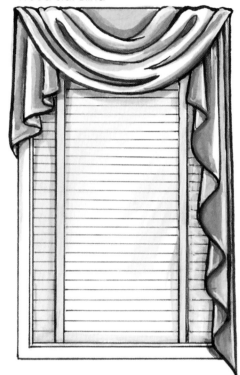

Miniblind. Narrow, $1/2$-inch-wide aluminum or PVC Venetian blinds are called miniblinds. They are particularly popular because when the blind is lowered and fully open, the slats are almost invisible. They come in a wide range of colors to match almost any decor. The 1-inch-wide blinds are also sometimes referred to as miniblinds.

Vertical Blind. Although vertical blinds are especially popular in offices, they are equally at home in a contemporary residential setting. They are installed on a track across the top of the window so that they can be drawn closed, just like draperies. Remote-control mechanisms are available so that they don't have to

Classic Venetian blinds *in this modern loft setting are easy to adjust when the homeowners want to maximize the view or minimize the amount of light.*

Miniblind

Vertical Blind

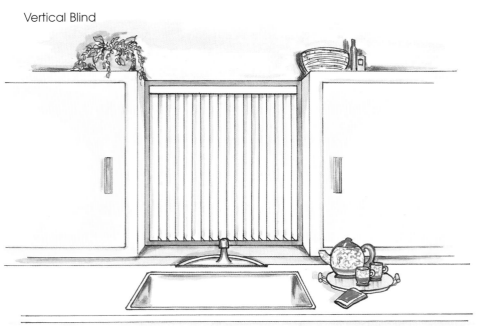

be closed by hand. The slats can be linked together at the bottom by a metal chain or left hanging free. The slats are commonly made from wood, synthetic flexible material, or stiffened fabric. Special track systems are available for bow, bay, and angled windows.

Window Shading. A special type of blind, called a *window shading,* features soft fabric slats inserted between two layers of sheer fabric, allowing daylight to filter through the open slats. Window shadings are available in horizontal and vertical styles. The fabric on the horizontal blinds lies flat; the vertical version falls in soft folds like pleated drapery.

Sunlight is diffused through a pair of window shadings, which are specialty blinds that consist of woven slats covered by two layers of sheer fabric.

By using only one full-length panel, the amount of framing is reduced for each planation shutter, which allows more natural light into the room. Because of the wide louvers, there is also a better view of the outdoors.

Shutters

Shutters conjure images of cozy interiors that envelop you in warmth and comfort. They can be installed inside the window frame on a mounting strip or outside the window opening in a frame of their own. Depending on the size of the window, they can be installed as a single shutter that swings open to one side of the window, as a pair that opens in the center, or as four or more panels that are hinged together and split at the center.

Shutters offer various options for privacy. Because they are good companions to almost any top treatment, they can be installed to cover the lower half of the window only. They are also a good buffer against noise, which makes them popular for street-level rooms in urban areas. When a window has two or more sets of shutters, a divider rail can be

Smart Tip

For the maximum the amount of light coming through shutters, use the largest panel possible on the window. Make sure the shutters have the same number of louvers per panel so that all of the windows in the room look unified. However, don't choose a panel that is over 48 inches high, because the shutter becomes unwieldy. Also, any window that is wider than 96 inches requires extra framing to support the shutters.

Alternating louvers and panels give these floor-to-ceiling shutters distinctive style. You can create custom shutters by mixing louvers and panels, as well as adjusting the louver widths.

installed so that the top half can open separately from the bottom. As a general rule, use the minimum number of panels possible to achieve the desired effect. More panels mean that more of the window is covered by the frames. Fewer panels will give you the most unobstructed view and allow you to control the light better.

Louvers are the vertical and horizontal slats that give shutters their character. Standard louver widths are $1^1/_4$, $1^3/_4$, $2^1/_2$, $3^1/_2$, and $4^1/_2$ inches. Wider louvers allow more sunlight into a room; narrow slats provide more screening.

MATERIALS

There are two materials that are used to make louvered and paneled shutters: wood and vinyl polymer.

Wood. Shutters are usually made of pine. Unfinished wood shutters can be stained or painted any color you desire; some styles are available prepainted in standard and custom colors. Wood shutters are a durable investment that enhances a home's value.

Vinyl. Vinyl polymer solves the problem of warping in bathrooms and other areas where there is steam and moisture. This material also wipes clean easily—a benefit in children's rooms and play areas. It is available in white and neutral colors.

Louver Shutters

There are three basic types of louver shutters: plantation, vertical, and café. If these don't suit your exact needs, be aware that shutters can be custom-fitted to specialty shaped windows, such as arches. However, with most of these unusual configurations, the louvers will not be movable.

Plantation Shutter. A shutter with a generous proportion is called a plantation shutter. For this style, the louvers are generally $2\frac{1}{2}$ to $4\frac{1}{2}$ inches wide and are set into panels that are 15 to 36 inches wide. Plantation shutters are frequently used in multiple sets, covering the entire window from top to bottom. They are also frequently used alone without any other window treatment. They can be installed as sliding panels, too—an arrangement that is suited to floor-length windows.

Vertical-Louver Shutter. This is a traditional shutter with louvers generally $1\frac{1}{4}$ inches wide and set in panels 8 to 12 inches wide. If you wish to mount it inside the window frame, you need a 2-inch clearance between the face of the window and the back of the shutter so that the louvers can open freely. If the distance is less than 2 inches, an outside mount will be required.

Café Shutter. This refers to the type of installation, rather than the style of the shutter. Like a café curtain, it is installed to cover half of the window. It can cover the lower half only, or a set can be double hung to cover the upper and lower halves of a window.

Café Shutters

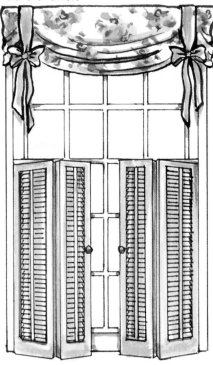

Vertical-Louver Shutters

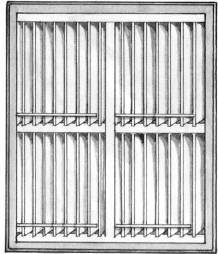

Don't rule out plantation shutters if your windows have an arch because a stationary type can be custom fitted.

More Shutter Styles

Strictly speaking, shutters can be any type of movable window covering that is set into a frame—a panel shutter is the most classic example of this. A fabric-insert shutter and a Shoji screen are other variations. No light passes through a closed panel shutter. However, a fabric-insert shutter or a Shoji screen diffuses light when closed

Panel Shutter. This consists of solid pieces of wood or interlocking strips of wood. It usually has some type of decoration, such as raised moldings or a stenciled design.

Fabric-Insert Shutter. This consists of panels of gathered fabric set into a wood frame. It can be used to create a more colorful look than traditional shutters. The fabric itself can be printed or plain, solid or lace; it can be selected to match the wallpaper or to repeat a fabric used elsewhere in the room. The best choices are light- to medium-weight fabrics that gather easily. Because a fabric panel is not lined, it can be damaged by sun, so choose a sun-resistant fabric.

Shoji Screen. This screen consists of a translucent panel set into a delicate wood frame. It usually slides open on a track, but it can also be hinged to work like a shutter. Often used as doors, shoji screens are also appropriate for windows. In traditional Japanese homes, the panels were originally made from rice paper. Today, panels are made from durable synthetic materials. This covering is compatible with both contemporary and Asian decor.

These fabric-insert café shutters have a blue-and-white fabric that coordinates with the room's curtains. When closed, only partial light comes through the shutters.

Shoji Screen

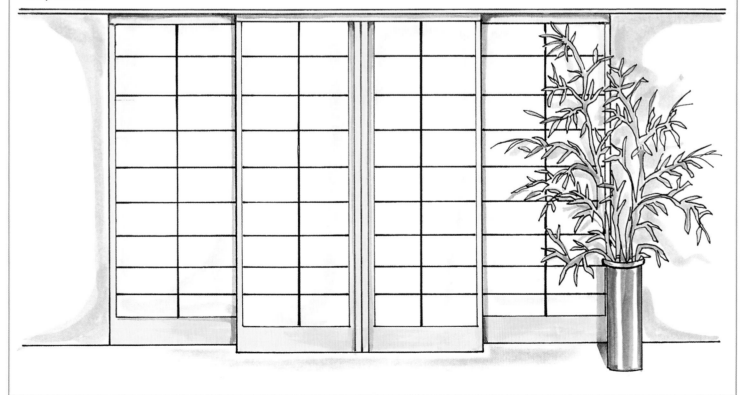

Cornices, Valances & Swags

Cornices, valances, and swags are all embellishments that enhance the persona of a room and add the finishing touch to virtually any style of window dressing. These top treatments can alter or emphasize the personality of the treatment underneath. For example, a ruffled valance can soften the linear qualities of shutters and blinds; a padded box cornice can complement the tailored character of vertical blinds; ornate swags and jabots can transform simple pleated drapery into an elaborately formal look; a tab valance can repeat the edge treatment of café curtains. Even a window with no under-treatment at all can benefit from the decorative punch that one of these window dressings provides. They add color and style without obstructing the view or blocking the light.

These top treatments have a practical purpose, too. They can cover up unsightly hardware and hide not-perfect headings. By mounting these treatments on the wall above a window, they can improve the appearance of imperfectly proportioned or mismatched windows. All of them can be mounted inside or outside the window frame, depending on the available wall space. However, a cornice is commonly installed as an outside mount. Placing a cornice inside the frame usually doesn't show off its shape to best advantage.

Bead-fringed swags with cascade tails unite four windows and create a focal point that frames a picturesque view in this elegant living room.

Swags & Jabots

Swags and jabots are purely decorative window treatments. We tend to think of them as gracing tall windows in stately country homes and elegant town houses, but they can be a beautiful addition to any room. Heavy fabrics, such as brocades and velvets, and elaborate trimmings are in keeping with their original formality. However, making them with lighter fabrics and simpler trimmings, as well as mating them with shutters or blinds, produces a less formal look.

Swags are the scallop-like shapes that extend across the top of the window. *Jabots* are the tails—softly pleated or shaped side panels with symmetrical or asymmetrical hemlines that flank a swag.

SMART STEPS

One: *Choose a symmetrical or asymmetrical arrangement.* In a symmetrical arrangement, the window treatment is the same on both sides of an imagined or real centerline. An example of a symmetrical arrangement is a series of three swags with matching jabots framing a picture window. The middle swag is positioned so that its center is exactly at the center of the window; one swag and one jabot flank it on each side. Because a symmetrical treatment appears formal, it looks appropriate in a traditional setting.

An asymmetrical arrangement refers to the balance between different-sized elements of a window treatment as a result of placement. For instance, a circular window can be dressed with a swag that has a long jabot (tail) on one side and a short one on the other. As long as the scale of the treatment is correct, the results will be quite pleasing.

Because an asymmetrical arrangement appears informal, it looks at home in a contemporary setting. But it can also work well in a traditional setting. Imagine a wall with a fireplace and two windows which are equal in size and distance from the fireplace. Each window could have a short jabot on its inside edge and a longer one on its outside edge. Individually, each window arrangement is asymmetrical. However, because they are mirror images of each other, the overall result is formal and symmetrical.

Two: *Determine the number of swags your window needs.* The size of the window affects how many swags are needed. As a general guideline,

Symmetrical arrangement: Each side of this swag-and-jabot treatment mirrors the other exactly, providing a classic example of well-balanced design.

With this asymmetrical scarf, the black-and-white border purposely emphasizes its uneven form. The tassels act as a visual counterbalance to the single, floor-length tail.

swags should be no more than 40 inches wide. The depth (or drop) of each swag generally ranges from 12 to 20 inches, depending on the height of the window.

Narrower windows look better with one or two swags. With more, the window treatment will look crowded. The swags should overlap slightly. If the swags are paired with a curtain or a blind, they should overlap enough to conceal the headings underneath. Wide windows require multiple swags to match their generous proportions. It is usually more attractive to use an uneven number of swags so that one full swag falls at the center of the window.

To help you decide how many swags you need, draw your window to scale on a piece of paper. Using tissue-paper overlays, sketch different arrangements of swags. When you find a pleasing one, drape lengths of string or cloth measuring tape across the top of your window to mimic the desired effect.

Three: ***Decide between formal and informal styles.*** This depends on several factors: the room's decor, the look you want to achieve, and the style of your curtains. Formal versions of swags and jabots are mounted on a board that is attached to the wall or the window frame. They are usually made from mid- to heavyweight fabrics, such as velvet,

brocade, or satin, and they are lined. Trimmings, including tassels and braids, can be opulent. Formal swags and jabots are usually paired with curtains and, sometimes, sheer inner curtains. Informal versions tend to be made from mid- to lightweight fabrics, such as chintz, linen, or voile. They often serve as top treatments for blinds and shutters. Informal swags and jabots may be mounted on a board but can also be hung from rods. Trimmings are applied with a light touch. Some informal swags are unlined and resemble scarves casually tossed over a pole.

Swags & Jabots

Although a swag-and-jabot arrangement looks as though it is made from one piece of material, each element is actually a series of separate sections. A *swag* can have a deep or a shallow drop. The deeper the drop, the fuller the folds.

A *fan swag*, which has folds that radiate out from the top center, is a variation of the traditional swag. Swags and jabots can also be hung on a rod with rings to form an apron-like effect over side curtains. Another variation foregoes the mounting board in favor of hidden hardware installed at the top of each jabot. This is particularly effective to create a crown-like design above a French door, where there are unusually high ceilings, or to enhance the illusion of a taller window.

Jabots are the tails of fabric that complement the swags. There is generally a jabot at each end of the treatment. However, for more visual interest, the treatment can also be designed with alternating swags and jabots. Plus, the jabot can lie under or over the ends of the swag.

Jabots are usually lined because the added weight helps them to hang better. If the underside of the tails are visible, a contrast lining is often used to accentuate the shape of the design.

The most common jabot style is the *cascade*, an asymmetrical tail that is created by fan-folding the fabric. When all the folds are arranged exactly on top of each other, the jabot falls in a narrow, stacked pattern. When the folds are staggered, the jabot is wider and the hemline undulates upwards. The other common

Fan Swag

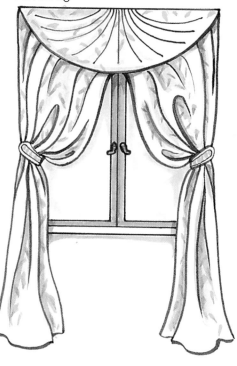

Swag on Curtain Rings

Here, a triple swag arrangement ends with rosettes, not jabots, for a more casual look. The contrasting fabrics of the curtains and the swags add dimension to the design.

Triple Swag & Cascade Jabot

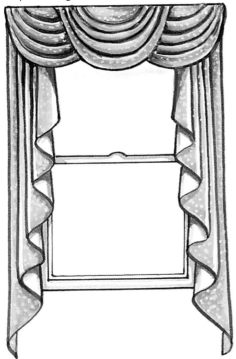

asymmetrical tail is the *spiral*—a corkscrew-like arrangement. Asymmetrical jabots are used in mirror-image at the ends of the treatment.

Symmetrical jabot styles include the *fluted jabot*, an open tube that curls to the underside, and the *pipe jabot*, a closed tube with a pointed hem. Symmetrical jabots are used at the center of the window, between the swags. They also can be used at each end in place of an asymmetrical tail.

Trimmings pair naturally with swags and jabots. The deep scoops of the swags and the undulating edges of the jabots often feature bullion and pom-pom fringe, cording, and ribbon borders. Rosettes, choux (ruched rosettes), Maltese crosses, and tassels can be added at the point where the swag is attached to the jabot.

A pair of double pipe jabots is highlighted by a lively plaid lining on this silk window dressing.

Crown Swag

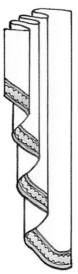

Cascade Jabot   Spiral Jabot   Fluted Jabot   Pipe Jabot

Scarf Swags

Scarf swags are a more relaxed interpretation of the swag-and-jabot treatment. They can be short, meaning sill length or shorter, or long, to the floor or gracefully puddling. Generally, a scarf treatment is created from one long piece of fabric. Lightweight fabrics with no right or wrong side, such as batiste, voile, lace, linen, and lawn, are particularly good choices because they fall into the soft folds that make this type of treatment so attractive.

Scarf treatments can be hung on poles, suspended from brackets, or tacked up with decorative hardware. Special brackets are also available to secure the fabric into various swag, tail, and rosette formations while remaining completely hidden from sight.

Scarf swags that are sill-length or shorter require some care to establish pleasing proportions. If the scarf is used alone, the tails should extend at least one-third of the way down the window. Otherwise, the end product tends to look a bit skimpy. Short scarves can also be

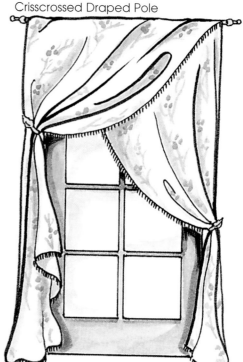

Crisscrossed Draped Pole

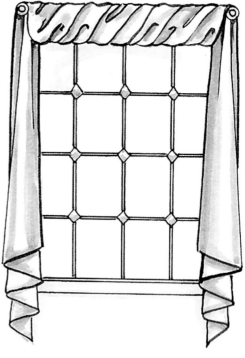

Wrapped Draped Pole

*This **wrapped long scarf** has full twists, accomplished through the combination of a midweight fabric and stuffing.*

installed over floor-length curtains to add drama to the window.

When a floor-length scarf is hung over a curtain rod, it is often referred to as a *draped pole*. These treatments can be tricky to hang simply because they use so much fabric. Puddling solves the problem of getting the hemline just right. Because they are heavier, long scarves also require more support than a short treatment. An asymmetrical style, with one long and one short tail, can be an interesting counterpoint to a window with an unusual shape.

Asymmetrical Draped Pole

Double Scarf Swag

Scarf Swag on Brackets

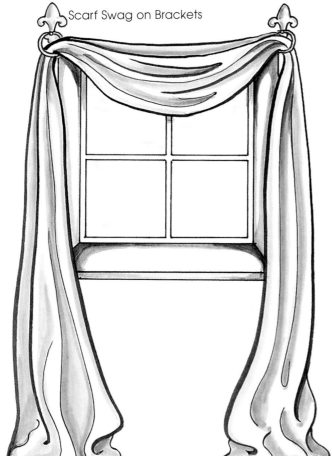

Sometimes simple is best. A basic, green-striped scarf, gathered on unobtrusive holdbacks, softens the wide profile of a double-hung window in a country cottage.

Valances

Valance is an all-encompassing term used for a range of treatments that are designed to be purely decorative. It is a soft fabric treatment, one that is usually draped, gathered, or folded. It covers no more than the upper third of the window glass, and generally covers much less. Valances can take many forms—from simple bands of fabric to elaborate arrangements with gathers and pleats. A valance can accompany drapery or stand alone.

While a valance does not contribute to privacy or light-blockage (except minimally), it does provide a way to add color and interest to a window, to visually balance curtains or shutters below, and to add another layer of decoration that can be enhanced by cords, gathers, pleats, and trim. From a practical point of view, it hides any unattractive hardware that belongs to underneath treatments, such as plain curtain rods and shade rollers. It also softens hard treatments, such as wood or metal blinds.

Proper Proportions. The valance should be in proportion to the window. This means that it should not be so long that it blocks the light or so short that it looks like a skimpy after-thought on the window. Longer windows mean longer valances. Valances are generally between 10 and 16 inches long, including the heading and any trim at the lower edge. Valances that involve generous swoops and folds of fabric,

such as some variations of the balloon valance, may be a little longer to accommodate the abundance of fabric. If the valance has tails, they should fall one-third of the way down the window.

Several other factors will influence the proportions of your valance. For an outside mount, the valance should be longer so that it extends to a pleasing point on the window glass. For an inside mount, the valance will be shorter. If your window has mullions or defined panes, avoid having the lower edge of the valance fall just short of a horizontal bar. The result will be an unattractive, chopped-off look. If the valance is installed over floor-length curtains, it should be longer so that it is in proportion to the expanse of fabric underneath. In this scenario, a valance with tails could be a dramatic topper extending one-third of the way down the draperies at the sides of the window.

Smart Tip

To determine the most pleasing proportion for your valance before making any purchases, try the brown-paper template technique. Cut some grocery bags apart or purchase brown kraft paper. Draw a template equal to the right length, and outline shape of your proposed valance. Cut out the template, and tape it in place across the top of your window. Analyze the proportions of the template. Is it too long? Too short? Make any necessary adjustments, and then note the final measurements.

Each scallop on this valance was generously sized to fit the width of one window in this set of narrow units. The arrangement gives the treatment a more tailored look.

When selecting a valance, choose a style that is compatible with your overall decor. For example, a gathered valance would look out of place in a contemporary setting, whereas a pleated or geometrically shaped one might be an excellent choice. Many pleated valances work well in formal settings, while balloon valances are frequently a good choice in a Victorian decor.

Hardware. The hardware for valances is as diversified as that for curtains. In some cases, the hardware and the style of the valance work together to create the overall effect. Decorative rods are a particularly good choice for tabbed valances. Clear rods are available for near-invisible hanging of lace and sheer valances. Double rods mean only one set of hardware for valance and draperies. Triple rods can accommodate an inner curtain, too. Some rods, such as wide Continental rods and those with arched tops, actually create the shape of the valance. Install the valance rod so that the sides of the valance extend slightly beyond any underneath treatment.

Styles. A valance can be pleated, gathered, shirred, or smooth. The fabric can match the rest of the window dressing, introduce a note of contrast, or repeat a fabric or color used elsewhere in the room. It can be hung on a decorative rod or a plain rod. The lower edge of the valance can be treated in a number of ways: it can be shaped, trimmed with a contrasting band, fringed, or adorned with a decorative edging, such as lace or braid. It can be longer at the sides than at the center. The upper edge can have looped cords, rosettes, bows, or tassels. These details, too, can be echoed elsewhere in the room, such as on a pillow.

For durability and to ensure that they hang properly, many valances are lined. However, light and breezy styles, such as those made from lace, voile, or other semitransparent fabrics, are not lined. A lining can also be eliminated if the valance is made from a particularly crisp fabric such as chintz or taffeta.

This flat valance, with its soft curves and tapered tails, uses an attention-getting sunny yellow fabric contrasted against a deep blue check. Note that the tails extend past the top third of the window.

Balloon Valances

A *balloon valance* gets its name from the fact that it has a full, puffed-out shape. Alone, it imparts a soft, somewhat feminine look to a window. In appearance, the basic balloon valance looks like a shorter version of the balloon shade, but it does not move up and down. Used with floor-length draperies, the effect is more formal. When designed with side tails, it has a tailored appearance.

A *puff valance* is a self-lined valance that is open at the ends so the two layers can be pulled apart to form a pouf. The *cloud valance* is similar to the balloon valance, but with more fullness at the lower edge of the scallops. The *Austrian valance* is shirred up into opulent scallops that fall along most of its length.

The deep scallops of a balloon valance in a sunroom are accentuated by the added detail of yellow ribbons.

Tailed Balloon Valance

Balloon Valance

Puff Valance

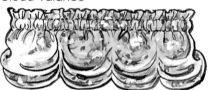

Cloud Valance

Austrian Valance

Pleated Valances

A *pleated valance* has a tailored, dressmaker look. Any of the headings that are commonly used for drapery can be applied to a pleated valance. The simplest version is the *box-pleat valance*, which looks like a schoolgirl's crisply pleated skirt. Other versions, such as the *triple-pleat* and *butterfly-pleat valances*, are pleated at the top and then released into soft folds. For the *pleated-and-gathered valance*, the area below the pleats is gathered up so that a series of swag-and-jabot-like shapes are formed. The *cartridge-pleat valance* consists of groupings of narrow, rounded pleats, spaced at intervals across the valance. On the *bell-pleat valance*, the unpressed pleats form soft cones of fabric.

*A **pleated-and-gathered valance** is a formal top treatment. In this inviting living room, the fancy valance is toned down by a cozy floral fabric.*

Box-Pleat Valance

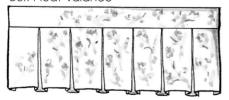

Triple-Pleat Valance

Bell-Pleat Valance

Pleated-and-Gathered Valance

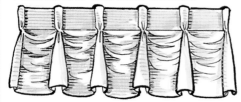

Cartridge-Pleat Valance

Butterfly-Pleat Valance

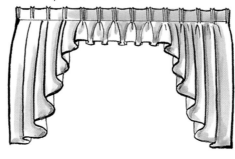

Tabbed Valances

With a *tabbed valance*, the drapery pole becomes an integral part of the window treatment. Because the tabs occur at intervals along the valance, this treatment is a wonderful way to showcase decorative rods and finials. (See Chapter 10, "Drapery Hardware," page 128.) Tabs can be made from wide or narrow strips of fabric, ribbon, or cord that complement or contrast with the main fabric of the curtain. They can also be left plain or decorated with details such as buttons, bows, and rosettes.

Hardware hangers, such as drapery rings or café clips, can substitute for the tabs. A flat valance, one that is the same width as the window, is called a *banner valance*. A fuller effect is created by selecting a valance that is at least one and a half times wider than the window.

*A **crenelated banner valance's** uncomplicated shape is in keeping with the simplicity of this old-fashioned bathroom.*

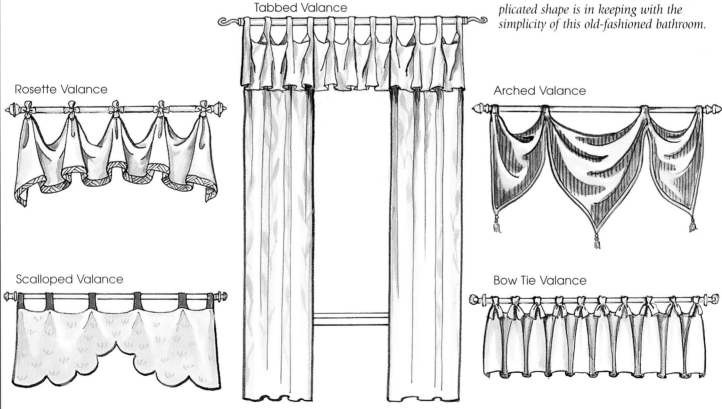

Rosette Valance

Tabbed Valance

Arched Valance

Scalloped Valance

Bow Tie Valance

Gathered Valances

The basic *gathered valance* is a long flat valance with a rod pocket. When it is shirred up on the rod, the gathers form. Generally, the flat valance is two to three times the width of the window. When using large amounts of material, a light-weight fabric is better because it creates a fuller effect.

Specialized standard curtain rods, such as wide Continental rods or arched rods, give the gathered valance a distinctive look. The *Federal valance* is created by pulling the ruffle up and securing it with a few stitches just below the rod pocket. Ruffled headers and shaped hemlines are another way to alter the look.

Federal Valance

Rod-Pocket Valance

Pointed Valance
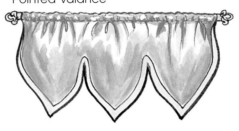

Arch-Top Valance
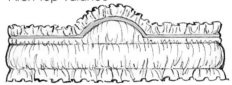

*A **simple gathered valance** shows this delicate print to its best advantage. The treatment was chosen to top the curtains because its loose folds don't obscure the bouquet-of-roses pattern.*

Cornices

Although cornices and valances are often mistaken for each other, a *cornice* is a more permanent arrangement. In fact, some cornices are elaborate wood structures that look like architectural elements. Others are upholstered or otherwise covered with fabric to coordinate with the decor.

Materials. Traditionally, cornices were wooden boxes that were painted or covered with fabric. Painted cornices often featured molding to heighten the architectural look of the treatments. Today, cornices are also made from buckram or cardboard attached to a cornice shelf or from a sturdy material such as foam core. Although these materials are stiff, they are easier to cut into curved and geometric shapes, expanding the variety of cornice designs.

The conventional box cornice has four sides: a face board (the front), two end boards (the sides), and a dust board (the top). The dust board helps deflect drafts—one reason why wood cornices were so popular in older homes.

Wooden box cornices can be painted or stained to match other woodwork in the room. They also provide a mounting place for indirect lighting, which can dramatically highlight the window treatment. Fabric coverings on wooden or foam-core box cornices can be padded, tufted, pleated, and outlined with piping for an upholstered look. Cornice shelves can have fabric attached along the edges of the shelf, with or without face board and end boards.

Scale. A cornice should balance the treatment and be in scale with the window. Because of its architectural nature, a cornice is always mounted outside the window, usually with the dust board or shelf aligned with the top of the frame. The cornice should be tall enough to cover the window's upper frame, plus the hardware and headings of any treatments underneath. Generally, cornices are $12^{1}/_{2}$ to 15 inches long. If the window is too short or the ceiling is very high, install the cornice on the wall above the window to create the illusion of height.

Cornices can be custom-made or purchased ready-made in standard sizes. Cornice kits are also available for easy assembly from lightweight panels of polystyrene; you supply the batting and the fabric. Whether you choose a cornice box or a cornice shelf as your base, there is a great range of styles available, as the following pages show.

Some cornices *are made of stiffened buckram and hung from a wood shelf. A red border and tassel shows off the sinuous shape of this fabric cornice.*

Shaped Cornices

Although a *shaped cornice* can be constructed from a cornice box, most use a cornice shelf. Buckram or cardboard—both easier than wood for cutting elaborately shaped designs—is attached to the shelf, serving as firm face- and end-board surfaces to be covered with fabric. The lower edge of a shaped cornice follows a geometric pattern. Scallops, inverted scallops, notches, and S-curves are common motifs. Piping or bands of trim can be used to emphasize the shape. A series of overlapping shapes, such as the triangles of the *pendant cornice,* can be individually reinforced and then attached to the cornice shelf. The cornice shelf can also support a painted or stained *wood crown* that extends above the shelf; a fabric ruffle is attached below it.

The cornices' intricate curves and scrolled corners echo the classic motifs on the period furniture in this parlor.

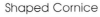
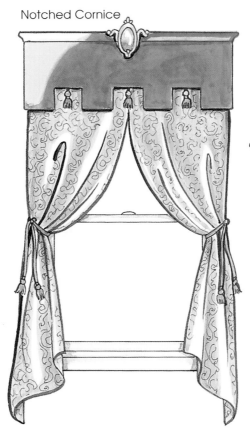
Notched Cornice

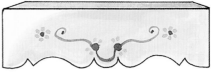
Shaped Cornice

Scalloped Cornice

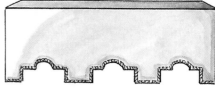
Cutout Cornice

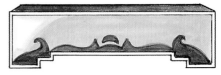
Geometric Cornice

Pendant Cornice

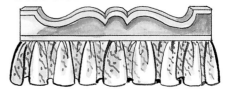
Wood Crown

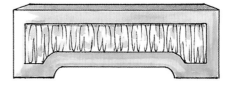
Fabric-Insert Cornice

Box Cornices

A *box cornice* provides a solid base for a variety of coverings. In general, a box-based cornice has more visual weight then one with a shelf base. Stained or painted wood-box cornices are embellished with architectural details, such as crown moldings, picture moldings, and carvings. This style is particularly appropriate for large, formal rooms, and it is an effective cover for curtain rods.

Upholstered box cornices are covered in mid- to heavyweight fabrics. The fabric can be applied so that the cornice has a smooth surface; it also can be manipulated into horizontal or vertical pleats or tufted with buttons or studs to give it

surface interest. Although sheers and lightweight fabrics are not appropriate for the base, they are lovely when used for hourglass, turban, smocked, swag, and other soft effects that are hung across the cornice.

The vintage wooden cornice in this Old World-style bedroom features egg-and-dart molding and gilded rosettes.

Pleated Cornice

Wood Cornice

Swagged Cornice

Hourglass Cornice

Turban Cornice

Mock Roman Cornice

Lambrequins

According to its traditional definition, a *lambrequin* is another name for a valance or a cornice. Today, however, it has come to mean a three-sided frame installed around the window—essentially a cornice with sides that extend down at least two-thirds of the window or to the floor. From a practical point of view, a lambrequin can conceal an unattractive window frame and help block excessive drafts. It also adds formality to the room. Because its long sides are subject to bumping and banging, a wood base, securely anchored to the window frame or wall, is best. A lambrequin can be upholstered, painted, or stained just like a box cornice. Moldings and painted details often echo other architectural elements in the room. Long, sheer draperies are frequent companions to lambrequins.

The lambrequins on these bay windows use visual trickery to add a whimsical note to the treatment. In keeping with the room's other faux elements, such as the columns on the walls, trompe l'oeil "valances" were painted onto the wood frames of the lambrequins.

Shaped Lambrequin

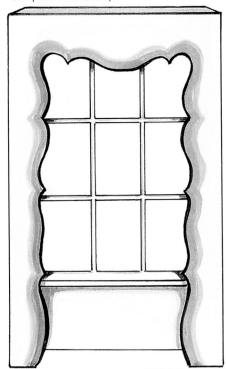

Arched Lambrequin

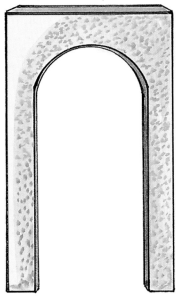

Tapered Lambrequin

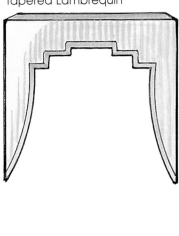

Choosing a Fabric

T he key to beautiful window decor is to use quality fabric. Good material will drape smoothly, pleat well, and have more body, which results in a professional-looking curtain. The more you know about how the fabric is made, the more successful you will be in choosing the right material. You should learn the fiber content of the yarn, how the cloth was dyed, and whether it has been treated with a special finish.

The weight of a fabric also contributes to the overall effect of a window dressing. Sheers soften the shape of the treatment and allow in light; opaque fabrics give an arrangement form and add warmth to a room. Patterns create visual variety, but it takes a practiced eye to mix more than one design together. Don't worry: You can learn to judge and combine the right colors and choose coordinating patterns in the right scale.

Once you start shopping for fabrics, the choices may seem overwhelming. But by examining samples on the basis of color and ability to drape, you can narrow your selections. After you've checked how the samples look in your home, you'll be ready to pick a fabric. The guidelines in this chapter will take you through the overall process, step by step.

*A **tapestry curtain** is a backdrop for an oval-backed chair covered in a toile de Jouy fabric. This unusual but effective pairing of materials works due to the large scale of the curtain's pattern in relation to that of the chair.*

A madras plaid was the right weight for these Roman blinds. This style calls for a fabric with some body to hold the folds.

weave, the yarns are alternated over and under each other, from side to side, and from top to bottom. This is the most common type of weave. A variation on the plain weave is the *ribbed weave*, which features a thick yarn over a thinner one. A *basket weave* uses two pieces of yarn for each row in a plain-weave pattern. A *twill weave* results in a herringbone pattern. A *satin weave* has a shiny smooth surface. A *pile weave* produces loops that are then cut to create a soft surface; velvet is a good example of this weave. A *Jacquard weave* requires a special loom that can do combinations of weaves, such as plain, twill, and satin.

A design can be woven into a fabric, becoming an integral part of it. Woven designs can be seen on the reverse side of the material. Some patterns are printed onto the surface of the cloth with dye, however. The color can seep through to the back of the material, but the design is blurred. Highly detailed printed fabrics can have as many as 20 or more colors.

Fabric Basics

Fabric consists of fibers that are natural—such as cotton or wool—or synthetic—such as rayon. When the fibers are spun (twisted), they become yarn. During the spinning process, natural and synthetic fibers can be blended, as in a cotton-polyester mix. Yarn quality depends on how tightly it is spun, how many strands of fiber are used, and the length of the fiber. To make fabric, yarns are then woven on a loom. Yarns used lengthwise on the loom are called warp; yarns that run widthwise are called weft. The same type of yarn can be made into a number of different weaves. For example, cotton can be woven into a damask or a canvas. For a *plain*

The colorfastness of dyes varies, an important factor with regard to window treatments. Fabric colors will fade due to constant exposure to the sun. Darker and brighter colors tend to fade faster than lighter, neutral colors. For the best resistance to sun damage, natural fibers should be vat-dyed and synthetic fibers should be solution-dyed. *Ask about the coloring process*. There are special finishes that can be applied to fabrics to help resist fading. There are also finishes to repel stains, mildew, and wrinkles, as well as fabrics with a sheen finish, such as that of glazed cotton (chintz).

A fabric's opacity influences how it will look in a room. Even if the color is dark, a sheer fabric or those with an open-weave create a soft effect and allow in light. Heavyweight fabrics, whether they are in a light or dark color, create a cozier atmosphere and keep out the sun.

Be aware that there is a difference between decorator fabrics and garment fabrics. Decorator fabrics have a higher thread count and are more tightly woven, so they will hold up better. Most are 54 inches wide, whereas garment fabrics are 45 inches wide. The wider the fabric, the less yardage you'll need for the treatment. But decorator fabrics are more costly.

COMMON FABRICS FOR WINDOW COVERINGS

Textiles play an important part when it comes to delivering color, pattern, and texture to a window dressing. Here is a brief overview of some common fabrics used to fabricate curtains, draperies and shades.

Brocade. Often a weighty fabric woven of silk, cotton, wool, or a combination. A raised, floral design in a Jacquard weave is its distinguishing feature. It is typically used for formal styles.

Cambric. A plain, tightly woven linen or cotton fabric with a sheen on one side. Curtain panels can be successfully made from it.

Canvas. A coarse, woven-cotton material available in heavy or lighter gauges. Canvas is strong and inexpensive. It works well for shades.

Chintz. Cotton fabric, often in a floral or other all-over print, is coated with a resin that gives it a sheen. Dry cleaning is necessary.

Cotton Duck. A cream-colored cotton that comes in various weights. It is ideal for no-sew curtains. (See canvas.)

Crewel. Plain woven, natural-cotton fabric with wool embroidery. Dry cleaning is required.

Chintz is a good choice for the medium weight needed for this pleated valance and straight draperies.

Damask. Another Jacquard material made of cotton, silk, wool, or a combination with a satin, raised design. This fabric is widely used for draperies.

Gingham. Plain-weave cotton fabric woven in block or checked prints. Its crisp look makes this fabric popular for borders and curtain panels.

Lace. Cotton or cotton-polyester blend material featuring an openwork design. Lace is favored for café curtains.

Linen. An unusually strong fabric made from processed flax. It's best when used in simple designs.

and through experimentation you will, too. Look through magazines for ideas. Remember, however, it is important to give your eyes a place to rest. Be sure to add a solid-color fabric or trimming into the mix as well.

Selecting a Fabric

Finding the right fabric is a matter of trial and error. Your first choice may not drape as well as you wanted or may come in only a too-dark color. To help the process go more smoothly, follow these steps.

SMART STEPS

One: ***Develop a color scheme.*** Now is the time to pick a color for your window covering. You can establish it based on elements that already exist in the room—an upholstered sofa, a carpet, or even a favorite painting. Once you determine the main color for the treatment, choose an accent or two. Accent colors can be used for border, trimmings, and even linings. (For more about color, see Chapter 3, "What's Your Decor?" page 34.) Collect samples of various fabrics and compare the colors until you find something that you like.

Two: ***Choose the right type of fabric for your window treatment.*** For the finished result to be successful, the fabric that you choose needs to suit the window treatment. Canvas is an excellent fabric for a shade, but it is too stiff to drape as a swag. A balloon shade needs a tightly woven material so that the scallops at the hem will hold their shapes and not sag. Don't judge a fabric by its looks alone; check the weight, weave, dyeing process, and how it should be cleaned. When you are using more than one type of fabric, make sure all of the materials are compatible in terms of weight and cleaning requirements. Ask yourself the following questions about any fabric you consider:

How durable is the fabric? If you expect to have your window covering a long time, this is an important question. Some

Floor-to-ceiling window treatments *require a heavy or lined fabric for the best pleats and draping.*

fabrics, such as silk, fade or deteriorate easily due to sun damage. To last, such materials need a lining or a special finish for protection.

Will the fabric drape well? This depends on the type of window dressing you want. Voile is often used for scarf swags because it is lightweight and hangs beautifully, but this sheer material may not have enough body for a pleated treatment. Thickly woven fabrics, such as tapestry, may be better suited to

straight panels rather than tieback ones. To learn how to assess a particular material's ability to drape, see the Smart Tip box below.

What type of cleaning will the fabric require? This goes back to the issue of maintenance, as was discussed in Chapter 4, page 44. If you don't want to fuss with your window dressing, you need an easy-care fabric. If you don't mind investing time—and money—in the upkeep of your arrangement, you have more options.

Is it treated with any special finishes? A special finish adds to the durability of a fabric. It can provide resistance to sun damage, mildew, and stains. Some finishes give the fabric more body for better draping.

Three: ***Check how the fabric looks in your home.*** Once you've narrowed down the choices, collect fabric samples. Because a small swatch may not show a complete pattern repeat, try to get the largest sample that you can. You may be able to borrow a large swatch from the fabric store. If not, buy a yard to take home. Hang the swatches next to the window on which you're planning to use them. Take note of the fabric's opacity during the day and in the evening when the lights are on. How do the colors hold up? Colors that look good in the evening may appear washed out in daylight. Once night falls, some dark colors can look muddy.

Delicate lace panels at a kitchen window soften the direct sunlight but allow a view to the outdoors.

Smart Tip

Test a fabric's draping ability by looking at a large piece in a fabric store. Gather at least two to three yards of material, holding one end in your hand. Check how it drapes. Does it fall into folds easily? Also look at the pattern when it is gathered. Does the design become lost in the folds? Ask a salesclerk or a friend to hold the fabric and look at it from a few feet away.

Decorative Embellishments

Once the basic curtain design is established, that's your cue to make the arrangement truly your own. The decorative embellishments that you select to accent the window decor reflect your personality and can give your design an individuality as unique as your own.

Decorative embellishments come in many forms. *Passementerie*—the French term for tassels and trimmings—encompasses a whole range of beautiful interlaced, braided, and fringed decorations that have traditionally been used to enhance window decor. Peaking during the Victorian era, passementerie has recently made a comeback—although now it is used with the refinement of the twentieth century and not the excessiveness of the nineteenth century.

Other accessories for curtains include tiebacks, borders, rosettes, and choux. The decorative potential of tiebacks is often taken for granted. Whether it is pleated, shaped, tied, or knotted, a tieback adds color and ornament to a treatment, as well as influencing its profile. Ruffled borders have always been consistently popular; appliquéd borders are a way of adding a custom motif to a drapery design. Rosettes and choux, in all their many forms, punctuate swags, scarves, valances, and even tiebacks.

Silk bullion fringe accents the shape of this swag-and-tail arrangement. Its golden color picks up the background hue of the curtain fabric.

Accessorizing Your Treatment

No window treatment is truly complete without embell-ishments. These decorations accent notable features, create intriguing profiles, and inject extra color into any arrange-ment. How do you pick the right ornament for your window decor? Follow these easy steps.

SMART STEPS

One: *Choose a color.* Tiebacks, ruffles, rosettes, and choux tend to be made from the same material as the curtain, but bor-ders, tassels, and trimmings can comple-ment or contrast the color of the face fabric. By choosing embellishments that subtly complement your window decor, you can enhance the entire effect. With patterned fabric, pull out a complementary hue from the design. With solid colors, try going one shade deeper for the embellishment. Contrasting the fabric color can be trickier to get right, but the results can be eye-catching.

Take a sample of the curtain fabric with you when you shop for tassels and trim-mings, so you will get the best color match or complement. Buy more than you need, not less: Should you come up short and need to purchase more, the dye from batch to batch will not match exactly. If you can't find the color that you want, some stores will custom-dye trimmings. However, many companies work with the trade (pro-fessionals) only, so you may have to purchase the embellishment through an interior designer.

Two: *Check the workmanship on tassels and trimmings.* Passementerie varies in quality—and in price. It can range from $2 to over $70 dollars for a tassel. Why is there such difference in price? It depends on whether the tassels and trimming are made by hand or machine. The type of thread used—such as silk, linen, viscose, cotton— also influences the cost. All passementerie

The color of trimmings and tassels affects the arrangement's overall design. Neutral embellishments subtly accent cream draperies.

Using the right proportions when adding trim to a design equals success. Here, a deep fringe balances out the valance, emphasizing it against the curtains.

should be evenly dyed and consistently smooth in appearance. When buying high-quality tassels, look for hand-tied pieces without any glue. Trimmings should not have loose threads along the top and bottom edges or breaks in the lengths.

Three: **Think about scale and proportion.** As was discussed in Chapter 2, page 20, scale and proportion are integral elements in designing a window treatment. This is no less true when choosing decorative embellishments. A 4-inch-wide flat braid may overwhelm a café curtain, but a $^1/_2$-inch border of ribbon may give it panache. Conversely, a rosette that is too small will look insignificant on an elaborate pleated-and-gathered valance. Trimmings and borders can emphasize an element by giving it visual weight. Bullion fringe will call attention to the conical shape of a pipe tail so that it doesn't go unnoticed on the swag.

Four: **Remember—less is more.** It is easy to overdo decorative embellishments. The point of these accessories is to enhance the window treatment, not overshadow it. If you are designing a formal arrangement, you want the effect to be sumptuous. Tasseled tiebacks on the panels and silk cording on the valance may look elegant; double-ruffles and tasseled tiebacks on the panels and rosettes, silk cording, and fan-edge fringe on the valance may be too busy, ruining the overall impression. If you prefer informal window dressings, keep embellishments to a minimum—one or two, at the most. For instance, if you are using prairie points on your shade, let that decoration stand alone. Add elements slowly and sparingly. A less costly way to test your choice is to make a quick sketch of the treatment.

Tiebacks

M ost window treatments look best when gracefully draped. Tiebacks are strips of fabric that gently hold back a curtain panel, giving it form and establishing the final shape of the arrangement. They also provide the opportunity to show off a window dressing's contrast lining.

Traditionally, tiebacks were made from fabric, ribbons, or rope with tassels. (For more information about tasseled tiebacks, see page 117 in this chapter.) But tiebacks can be successfully fabricated from such imaginative materials as ribbon-covered hairclips, strings of beads, scarves, and belts.

To hang tiebacks, attach a small hook to the wall at the appropriate height. (Other options include using ornate holdbacks and concealed-tieback holders; see Chapter 10, "Drapery Hardware," on page 130.) Sew metal rings or fabric loops onto the ends of the tieback, and then fasten them onto the hook.

Bow Tieback

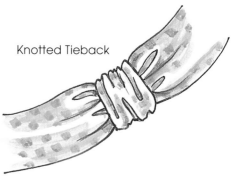

Knotted Tieback

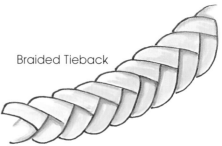

Braided Tieback

*A **bow tieback** was made from the same iridescent fabric as the curtain. It gives the treatment a unified look.*

Crescent tiebacks in solid beige match the tabs on these tapestry curtains. Buttons cover the areas where the tiebacks are attached to wall hooks.

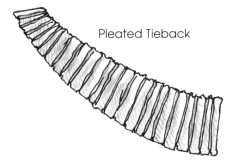

Pleated Tieback

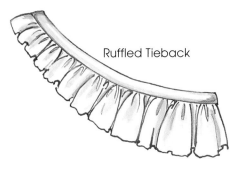

Ruffled Tieback

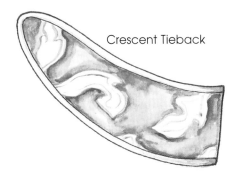

Crescent Tieback

Fabric Tieback. This is a narrow strip of curtain material that is lined. For a *bow* tieback, you literally tie a strip of fabric or a ribbon in a bow onto the curtain. Or you can use a loop of fabric with a pre-made bow attached. You can position the bow toward the front, side, or back of the panel. A *knotted* tieback is simply tied in the center, creating a decorative but unobtrusive accessory. A *braided* tieback consists of three strips of fabric that are plaited. It can also be made of welting (fabric-covered cording) for a fuller, puffier effect.

You can fashion a tieback from *pencil pleats*, too. Make sure to have a buckram backing so that the pleats hold their shape. You can also trim fabric tieback with a *ruffle*.

Shaped Tieback. A template is used to establish the basic shape of the tieback. Some popular shapes are crescents, scallops, and rectangles with round corners. A shaped tieback is stiffened by a buckram backing. Although a shaped tieback is usually made to match the curtain fabric, it can be adorned with piping, rosettes, or buttons.

Ruffles & Borders

Ruffles and borders are attractive ways to finish off the edge of a curtain or the hem of a shade. Like other embellishments, these edgings add definition to a treatment's shape.

Prairie Points. This features small squares of material placed at an angle to the edge of the curtain fabric, resulting in a zigzag border.

Ruffles. A ruffle is a border of gathered fabric attached to the edge of a curtain or shade. A *double ruffle* features two layers of frill. A *pleated ruffle* falls in neat folds.

Borders. This can be as simple as an attractive ribbon or a piece of contrasting fabric attached to the edge of a treatment. *Appliquéd borders* are cutout patterns sewn onto the edge of a curtain or shade. Some of the motifs include waves, leaves, Greek key patterns, and geometric designs.

Prairie points in bold colors of lime, grape, and lemon echo the zigzag pattern painted on the walls of this modern sitting room.

Prairie Points

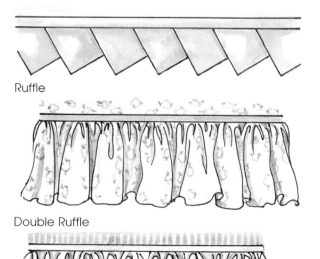

Ruffle

Double Ruffle

Pleated Ruffle

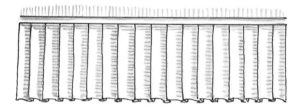

Appliquéd Border

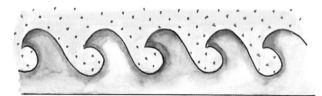

Tassels

A tassel is the purist form of embell-ishment—decoration for decora-tion's sake. Consisting of a head and a skirt, a tassel is typically made of silk, cotton, linen, or wool. Other materials, such as jute or beading, are also used.

The tassel's head is constructed from a wooden form or bead covered with thread and tatting (a lace of looped and knotted thread). Flat, dome, ball, arrow, or rectangular forms can be used to shape the head. The skirt extends below the head and can be made of bullion fringe or cut or looped yarn.

A dangling tassel draws the eye to what-ever feature it is accenting. It is often centered on a valance or a swag; it can also punctuate the notches of a cornice. A tassel can be a visual counterbalance to the long tail of an asymmetrical treat-ment. Or it can function as a shade pull. When you attach a tassel to a thick cord, it becomes a luxurious tieback.

Frog Tassel

Key Tassel. A traditional type of tassel that was formerly used on key fobs.

Rosette. In this case, the rosette is a circular ornament of tatting, painted wood, or semi-precious stone baubles with a tassel attached.

Frog Tassel. It has three loops of cording with a rosette in the center. The tassels hang from cording behind the rosette.

Beaded Tassel

Key Tassel

*A **tasseled tieback** in vivid red, green, and gold holds its own against the deep colors of an oversized floral print.*

Choux & Rosettes

Choux and rosettes usually adorn multilayered window dressings and swags, but they also embellish tiebacks. These decorations highlight any spot on which they are placed, so choose their location wisely.

Choux. This projects out farther than other finishing touches, so it is more noticeable. With a small piece of buckram as a backing, a circle of fabric is gathered and secured randomly, creating a ruched ball. For scarves, there is an easier and less formal way to make a choux: The fabric is knotted.

Maltese Cross. Made of curtain fabric or ribbon, this bow consists of four loops and no tails. The center of the cross is disguised by a small circle of material or a fabric-covered button. It is a more informal decoration than the others.

A knife-pleated rosette disguises the point where the swag meets the curtain.

Choux

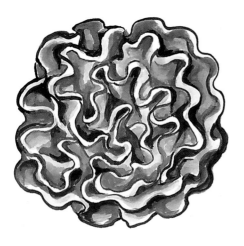

Maltese Cross

Fabric Rose

Fabric Rose. Often made with wire ribbon, the material is gathered and secured from the center outward, creating a spiral of fabric.

Ruffle Rosette. This flower-like embellishment features a tightly gathered center with a loosely ruffled edge.

Knife-Pleated Rosette. For this tailored effect, the material is pleated and the ends are joined to make a circle. A fabric-covered disc is attached to the center of the rosette.

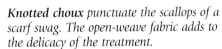

Ruffle Rosette

Knife-Pleated Rosette

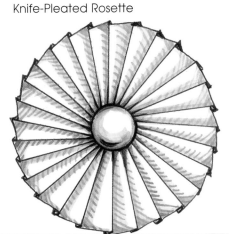

Knotted choux punctuate the scallops of a scarf swag. The open-weave fabric adds to the delicacy of the treatment.

Trimmings

Trimmings cover a variety of border-like edgings that are used to embellish curtains. This category encompasses gimps, braids, picot braids, piping, cording, jacquard borders, and fringes. Originally designed to cover seams and edges, these borders add definition to the shape of a treatment. For instance, the edge of a cascade jabot can be highlighted by fringe.

Trimmings are woven from fibers, such as wool, silk, cotton, or gold or silver threads. They can also be fabricated from other less-typical materials, such as chenille, organdy, or hemp. Fringes, in particular, can feature beading, feathers, or stone baubles.

Picot Braid. This flat braid has a pattern of small loops or scallops projecting from the side of the border.

Gimp. A ribbon-like braid of silk or cotton that is stiffened with a wire.

Flat Braid. Also known as a galloon, this can be woven in any fiber. It ranges in size from $1^1/_2$ to 3 inches wide.

Cording. Yarn is twisted together to make a cord. Thick cording is used for tiebacks with tassels.

Jacquard Border. A flat border woven on a Jacquard loom. It can be $2^1/_2$ to 6 inches wide.

Picot Braid

Flat Braid

Cording with Selvage

Jacquard Border

The custom-died fringe featured on these formal curtains have pom-poms that coordinate with the colors of the yellow check fabric.

Fan-Edge Braid. This has small looped cords in an undulating pattern.

Piping. Also called welting, this is a strip of fabric folded over a cord. Although it is available ready-made, it can be sewn by hand.

Fringe. This has a skirt of twisted cords topped by a braid, lace, or crochet-work heading. The skirt can be ornamented by tassels, teardrops (fabric-covered balls), tufting (a cluster of threads), and beading. *Brush fringe* has a row of cut cords. Originally made of gold or silver thread, *bullion fringe* features thick, twisted cords. *Campaign fringe* has one or more rows of of bell-shaped tassels; its name comes from the Italian word *campana*, meaning bell. *Tasseled fringe* ties together sections of the cord at even intervals. *Looped fringe* leaves the twisted cords uncut.

Fringe should never overwhelm a design. Delicate glass-bead fringe complements the airy sheer fabric of these balloon shades.

Fan-Edge Braid

Brush Fringe

Bullion Fringe

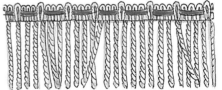

Campaign Fringe

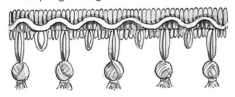

Tasseled Fringe

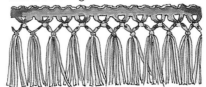

Looped Fringe

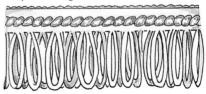

Drapery Hardware

When thinking of drapery hardware, a standard traverse rod or a basic pole with brackets comes to mind for most homeowners—and rightfully so, because drapery hardware is the most functional element of a window treatment. Many types of supports are designed to remain unseen, allowing the curtains to draw all the attention. But other types are meant to be visible, offering decorative impact as well.

In fact, you can think of some drapery hardware as jewelry for your windows. Finials, holdbacks, drapery pins, and swag holders come in an endless array of motifs—from suns and fleur-de-lis to curlicues and ram's heads. Even rods and poles have decorative possibilities. They are available in a variety of materials, including metals (brass, cast and wrought iron, steel, and gold- and nickel-plated), plastic, and wood. Faux finishes, such as verdegris and marbling, are also favorite ways to customize fittings.

If your drapery hardware will be visible, you can choose a style that complements the curtain's design, but contrasting it can be equally effective. For instance, if the treatment is a tabbed curtain in a sheer fabric, you can play against the delicacy of the fabric by choosing a narrow, wrought-iron pole with a shepard's crook finial.

Wrought-iron poles with scrolled finials were custom-made for these windows. The window dressings were purposely played down to show off the hardware.

Café clips are a quick and easy way to hang lightweight curtains with a plain heading. The clips often feature decorative motifs, such as suns and stars.

Choosing Hardware

Before you can choose your hardware, you have to evaluate your window and the window decor you're planning to use. Will the treatment be installed inside or outside the window frame? Each situation calls for a different type of drapery hardware. An inside mount needs a rod or a pole that fits within the frame of the window. Suggestions include a basic traverse rod, a ceiling-mounted rod, a swivel rod, and a tension rod. There are no restrictions with an outside mount, so you can use any style of drapery hardware. However, when a window is poorly located, there are exceptions. A window that is too close to the ceiling requires ceiling-mounted

Smart Tip

Although it is rarely noticed, a bracket plays an important role in supporting rods and poles. If a treatment rubs against a window frame, an extension bracket solves the problem. It projects from the wall at an adjustable length, providing enough clearance. A hold-down bracket anchors a cellular shade or a blind to the bottom of a door, preventing the treatment from moving when the door is opened or closed.

hardware. Corner windows or a window close to a corner are other problem spots. Stay clear of using a pole with large, ornate finials; it won't fit in these situations. Stick to an expandable traverse rod for curtains or swag holders for scarves because neither takes up much space.

Is the treatment stationary? Or is it movable? Again, the hardware should suit the situation. For a stationary treatment, try a continental rod or a pole with finials. Traverse rods are the best for movable treatments. You can decide between a one-way or a two-way draw. A one-way draw pulls the curtain in one direction—either right or left. A two-way type draws the panels in opposite directions. The *headrail* anchors a shade or a blind, and it is the location for the track (if there is one). Vertical blinds can be drawn to one side or can split in the middle. The latter is known as a *split headrail* because, like a two-way traverse rod, each half of the treatment moves in a different direction. A two-on-one headrail features two cellular shades on one head-rail, which is ideal for wide windows or sliding glass doors.

Will the hardware be seen? Or will it remain hidden? This also influences your choices. When the hardware will be shown off, a pole with finials is the most decorative option. But if your design requires easy operation, a concealed-track rod may work for you. If the hardware will remain unseen, go with a traverse rod. It will allow you to move the curtain easily and can be tucked away under a valance or cornice.

OPERATING CONTROLS

There are different types of operating controls for window treatments. A *cording system* is the most common means of moving a treatment, but it varies with the style of the window decor. For instance, a cord pulley on a traverse rod draws curtains aside. For some shades, a system of rings and cords pulls the fabric up and down. In the case of vertical blinds, a chain system with a wheel mechanism moves the slats from side to side as well as adjusts their angle. For any of these, you can choose which side of the treatment to hang the cording system.

A wand is another way to draw window dressings, particularly vertical blinds. Basically, it's a plastic pole that hangs from one side of an arrangement, in place of the cording. When drawn by hand, the wand pushes the treatment along the track. When the wand for vertical blinds is twisted, it rotates the slats to any angle you desire.

Plan ahead where you want the operating controls to be located. In general, put an operating control on the side where you have the best access and where it is the least visible. If there is a cording system and a wand, keep both controls on the same side of the treatment. For corner windows, don't place operating controls in the middle—it will look cluttered. Place the cording system or wands on the left for the left window and on the right for the right unit.

Knobs or pegs are an alternative to traditional drapery hardware. This blue gingham curtain was simply hung by corded loops, giving the treatment country charm.

Curtain Rods

A curtain rod is the most functional means of supporting a window dressing. Because a curtain rod features a track system, it is the easiest type of drapery hardware to operate. The system consists of plastic or brass runners that glide along the track. Brackets are attached to the wall to hold the track (unless it is ceiling mounted). Usually, a cord pulley adjusts the runners, but some are moved by hand. Typically, a curtain rod is utilitarian looking, not decorative. If the curtain's heading won't be shown, the rod is often hidden behind a valance, cornice, or swag.

Expandable Traverse Rod

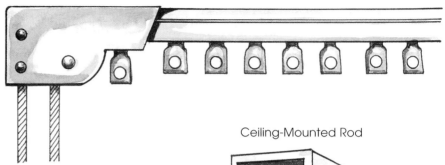

A concealed-track rod used on bay windows has to be professionally installed because it must be curved to fit the location. Here, a double curtain rod was used so that the inner and outer draperies could be moved separately.

Ceiling-Mounted Rod

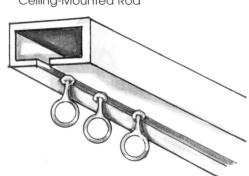

Tension Rod. A rubber-tipped rod with a spring mechanism that holds it in place within the window frame; it is useful for recessed windows. Lightweight curtains are the only option.

Standard Traverse Rod. There are two types of this rod: a basic track and an expandable version. A traverse rod is concealed when the curtains are closed. It is available with one-way and two-way draw. This rod can be bent by a professional for a bow window installation.

Ceiling-Mounted Rod. Instead of having brackets, this rod attaches to the ceiling or underneath the top of the window frame. It works well in a tight space, such as a dormer window.

Continental Rod. This stationary rod is $2\,^{1}/_{2}$ to $4\,^{1}/_{2}$ inches wide. It creates a deep heading on rod-pocket curtains, giving them visual interest. It is also used to make a rod sleeve more valance-like.

Double-Track Rod

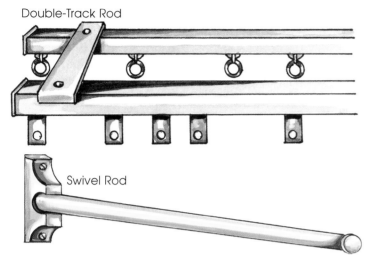

Track-and-Valance Rod

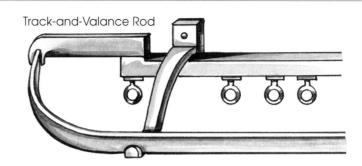

Swivel Rod

Wire hardware is useful in situations where there are corner windows or a curved bay because the wire bends easily and is supported at intervals by brackets.

Concealed-Track Rod. This is a hybrid between a rod and a pole. The front is a semicircular shape that looks like a pole; in back, there is a hidden track with a cording system.

Double-Track Rod. Useful for layered treatments, this provides two tracks for inner and outer curtains. Each track has its own cord pulley. A triple-track version, for two curtains and a valance, is also available.

Track-and-Valance Rod. This hangs a curtain and a valance on the same fitting. A rail for the stationary valance projects in front of a traverse rod for the drapery.

Swivel Rod. Handy where there is no stack-back space, this fitting is hinged so that it swings away from the window when opened. It works best on small windows, particularly recessed ones.

Wire Rod. This consists of metal wire threaded through small brackets. It can be easily used for bow, bay, and corner windows. Choose mid- to lightweight treatments, not heavy ones.

Poles & Finials

Because of its decorative nature, a pole with finials can command as much attention as a window dressing. A pole is fixed to a window by brackets. (Use sockets for inside mounts.) Unless it's a tabbed or rod-pocket curtain, the treatment will require curtain rings or café clips to hang from the pole. These usually match the material and finish of the support. Café clips can be adorned with motifs such as stars or leaves.

Wooden Poles. The types of wood range from the inexpensive (pine and beech) to the expensive (mahogany and ebony). It can be left unfinished, stained, or painted. Finishes include metallic, verdegris, gilt, and faux marble. The pole can be turned to feature fluting (rounded grooves). To make rings glide smoothly, use silicone spray on the top of the pole.

A marbled pole with a gilded finial and decorative bracket matches the sophistication of an arched valance.

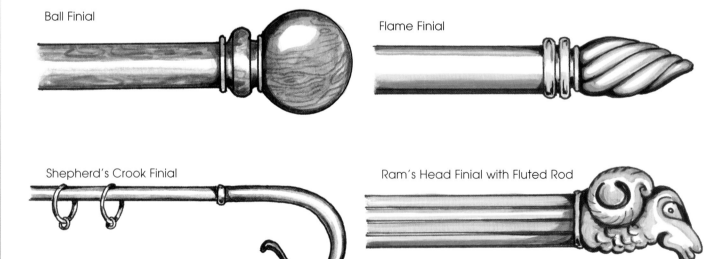

Ball Finial

Flame Finial

Shepherd's Crook Finial

Ram's Head Finial with Fluted Rod

Custom finials, such as these delicate leaf ones, are a way to include a unique element in your decorating scheme.

Metal Poles. Brass, wrought iron, and steel are the most common metals used for this support. The diameter of the pole can range from narrow café style to wide cornice poles.

Finials. This decorative end to the pole comes in standard or custom-made motifs. It can be made of brass, copper, wrought iron, glass, ceramic, or wood. Some classic motifs for finials are scrolls, balls, shepherd's crooks, flames, ram's heads (and other animals), leaves, and arrowheads. For a creative touch, some finials can be turned into pegs for hanging curtains from the ceiling.

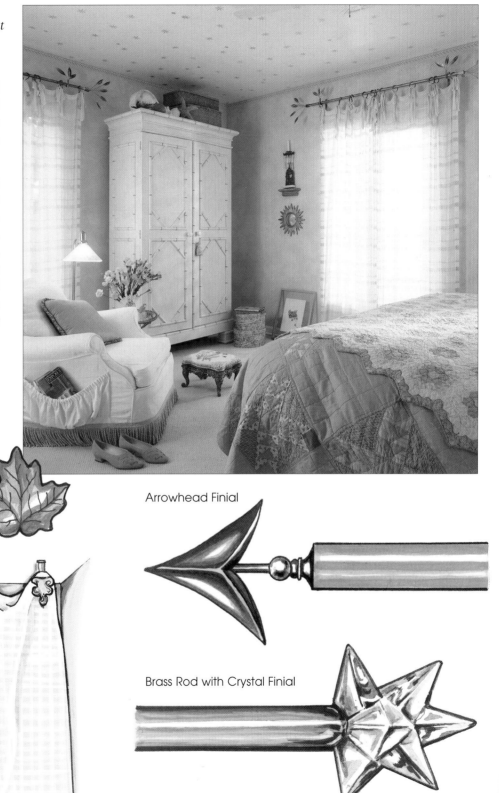

Café Clips

Ceiling-Mounted Clips

Arrowhead Finial

Brass Rod with Crystal Finial

Holdbacks

Holdbacks are multipurpose drapery hardware. Traditionally, a holdback is used in place of a fabric tieback. It is attached to the wall, near the edge of the window frame, and the curtain is caught behind it. For a sumptuous look, a tasseled tieback can be hooked on the holdback. When placed at the top of the window, a holdback can also function as a swag holder. Holdbacks can be made of metal, wood, or glass. Design motifs include rosettes, shells, flowers, curlicues, scrolls, and hearts. A *concealed tieback holder* is an adjustable plastic piece that holds the curtain away from the wall, preventing a tieback from creasing the fabric. It is not visible.

*A **wrought-iron holdback** with scrolled ends catches a white ruffled curtain.*

Basic Holdbacks

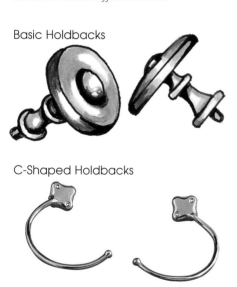

C-Shaped Holdbacks

Floral Holdbacks

Seashell Holdbacks

Dogwood Holdbacks

Glass Holdbacks

Other Hardware

Drapery pins and swag holders are decorative accents for curtains. *Drapery pins* add detail to your window dressing. Used on lightweight curtains, the metal pins hold back a small amount of fabric. A *swag holder* is akin to a holdback, except with a looped piece of metal in which the swag is hung. Another type of swag holder looks like a plaster corbel (a projecting bracket) with an opening for the swag.

If you don't see the drapery hardware you want, or if you have your own idea, have a custom fitting made. You will need to work with an interior designer who has access to custom sources. Doing so is expensive, however.

Drapery Pins

Plaster Swag Holder

Custom Bracket

Metal swagholders are used to create a crown swag over a French door and windows. The holders are fastened to the wall or the window's woodwork.

Problem Solving

Sooner or later, we are all faced with a common decorating predicament: the window that just doesn't conform to the rules (or the room). It might be too tall or too short, too narrow or too wide. It might be an expansive wall of windows or a cozy bay arrangement. A small window tucked up high or a large window that extends all the way to the ceiling can be difficult to treat. Two windows that seem to crash into each other at a corner can be confounding, too. An interesting shape that is out of harmony with the rest of the room might be your problem. Or maybe you have a window that is just plain ugly.

Take heart! No matter what the difficulty is, there is a way around it. The solution varies according to the restrictions imposed by the window itself, the surrounding decor, your lifestyle, your budget, and your imagination— which is what this chapter is all about.

In the pages that follow, common problems are identified. Solutions are proposed for mismatched windows, windows in difficult locations, and other challenges, such as large sizes, special shapes, glazed doors, dormers, and corner units. And, even if your situation is not addressed, our three-step decision-making process, plus the knowledge from the previous chapters, will give you the tools to turn any problem window into a decorating asset.

Turn a problem area into eye-catching showpiece: Corner windows are given a dramatic treatment of back-to-back sheers on decorative hardware.

These tall, narrow windows overwhelmed this small sitting room. Puff valances visually lower the scale of the windows without blocking the sunlight.

little bit of thought and imagination to come up with satisfying solutions.

SMART STEPS

One: **Assess the problem.** Is it the shape and size of the window that is causing the problem? Some windows are visually too short and wide for a room; others are too tall and narrow. Occasionally, mismatched windows end up side by side on the same wall or on adjacent walls. This is common in many older ranch-style houses where the bedrooms have standard-size windows and small, crank-operated awning windows. Some windows are just in difficult locations because of architectural changes, such as when a room has been divided or a ceiling has been dropped. Is there a window that's too close to a wall? Or one that abuts the ceiling? Dressing windows in large sizes can also be a difficulty, particularly when you have two competing goals, such as privacy and light. Many of today's large homes have media/family rooms with a fireplace, a wall of windows, and no place to put the television without contending with the glare. Unusual shapes can also be difficult. Cathedral windows, Palladians, arched units, ovals, triangles, glazed doors, skylights, and dormer windows all present challenges—ones that can be compounded by the size and shape of other windows in the room.

Designs for Difficult Windows

Sometimes windows are in locations that are difficult to treat. Or there may be one window that is out of place in terms of the size and style of other windows in the room.

There are many reasons why this can happen. Perhaps when the house was first built, its outside appearance took precedence over inside consistency. Or it has a new addition with windows that don't match the old ones. Or if old windows had to be replaced, local fire codes may have dictated a different size. Or an attic with dormer windows, originally intended for storage, has been transformed into an extra bedroom or a home office. In these situations, all it takes is a

Two: **Identify your needs.** With your notes from Chapter 4, review what you need from the window treatments. Is there too much light in the room? Not enough? A window treatment in lively colors can help dispel the gloom in a room that is shaded from the sun by trees or other buildings.

Think about what you can see from the windows. Do you want to cover an unattractive view? Or is the view one of the reasons you moved there in the first place? Is privacy a priority? Daytime privacy? Nighttime privacy? Or both? think about how others see your windows. Large windows should be treated in a style that is compatible with the other windows on the same elevation. This is particularly important when the window is at the front of the house where passers-by have a curbside view.

Is the window accessible? Lack of access can make cleaning a problem with a very large window or a window in a hard-to-reach location. What is your budget? Even difficult windows have more than one solution. You want to find ones that are within your budget, in terms of both initial expenditure and maintenance costs.

Three: *Look for inspiration.* No matter what problem you encounter, there's a window treatment that provides the desired solution. In Chapters 5, 6, and 7 (pages 48–84), you became familiar with all the elements that comprise a total window treatment. The only limit to the number of ways these elements can be combined is your imagination. But sometimes imagination needs a bit of help. You can, of course, always call in the professionals, but even if you plan to do that, it helps if you have some idea of what direction you want to take. Study the photographs in this book; then flip through the pages of decorating magazines. Try to look beyond the treatments themselves to imagine the framework of the windows. Look for windows with the proportions, locations, or shapes that match the challenges you are facing.

A group of small windows didn't have enough decorative impact for this dining room. To create a focal point, the valance is placed on the wall above the window, and the curtains extend past the frame.

Mismatched Window Sizes

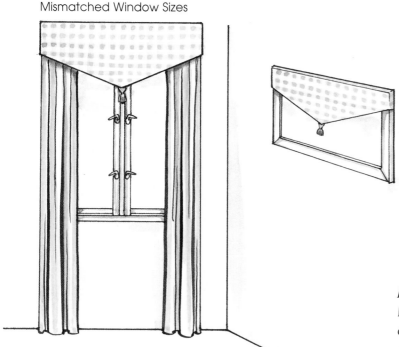

window frame. For an individual window that looks too short, try the same trick—place the curtain rod high on the wall, and hang floor-length panels. Even if you are using tabbed curtains rather than a formal arrangement, the two long curtain panels draw the eye upward, offsetting the short window. If the rod is visible, make sure the hardware is attractive or the finish ties in with the decor. Wide windows require different measures. To visually reduce the width, consider a floor-length curtain in a color that matches the walls to play down the horizontal form. Position the curtain so that it covers part of the window. Or consider a series of Roman or cascade shades to break up the horizontal line; the effect is increased if you adjust each shade to a different level.

MISMATCHED WINDOWS

Mismatched windows in a room are windows unlike each other in size or shape and lack any distinctive features that distinguish them as an architectural focal point. The goal is to make these windows appear as similar as possible.

Mismatched Size. If the size difference is not too great, install a valance or cornice above all of the windows at the same height. This may mean mounting a heading on the wall above a window. Use an outside mount to disguise the position of the frames. Mount shades or blinds directly under the header. If there is a big difference, plan the larger window first, and then scale the treatment down for the smaller window.

Mismatched Shape. You can choose a different treatment for each window in this situation, but use the same fabrics. You can also link them by using the same hardware.

DIFFICULT LOCATIONS

Sometimes a window is situated in such a way that there is little room above or to the sides of the frame, or the window may be in a hard-to-get-at spot—a skylight, for example. Despite the location, aesthetics, privacy, or light control may necessitate some type of coverage.

Window Close to a Corner. When one of two windows is too close to a corner, choose a treatment that doesn't have to

POOR PROPORTIONS

Proportion is a design element that is important to all the components of a room. When a window is too tall, too narrow, too wide, or too short, it throws off the room's entire design. Fortunately, window treatments are a fabulous way to camouflage any of these flaws without the expense and upheaval of replacing the offending window.

Tall and Narrow. Though tall windows are desirable in most cases, certain styles can run too high and appear too narrow, adding an unwanted element to your room's design. For windows that are too tall, use a cornice or a valance to visually lower the length of the opening. If your window is too narrow, extend the curtains past the window frame, covering some of the wall. With shades or blinds, choose an outside mount to make the window seem wider.

Short and Wide. Some rooms call for dramatic windows. For instance, a formal dining room may have a group of small sash windows that seem insignificant in the scheme. To visually enlarge them, run a valance or cornice above the top of the window, and extend the curtains past the stack back. Blinds with a swag offer a functional yet decorative approach. Other ideas include café curtains with simple valances or sill-length tab curtains mounted inside the window frame. For a single window, consider emphasizing the asymmetry with a curtain that is tied back to one side.

Window Close to the Ceiling. Because there isn't any wall space for the rod or track hardware, use ceiling hardware, or mount a lath onto the ceiling to support the rod or track and cover it with a cornice. If you choose ceiling hardware, remember that the curtains will be stationary. Keep the style simple and the fabric lightweight because the hardware won't withstand heavier treatments. Or consider a cornice, which blocks the top of the window, helping to visually lower it.

Skylights. Most skylights are installed to increase light, so they are rarely covered. Sometimes, however, light is too glaring or makes the space too warm. A cellular shade with side-tracks to hold it flush against the window is a good solution. If the shade is easily reached, it can be moved by hand. Otherwise, a telescoping pole or electronic control is required.

A casual solution, which uses woven blinds, works best where there is a series of skylights, such as in a garden room. Mount the blind at the top of the skylight. Run cording down both sides of the skylight and through rings that have been attached to each end of the blind's hem. When lowered, the blind bows gently in the center, so leave enough above-head clearance.

CHALLENGING WINDOWS
Some windows present their own particular challenges because of their style or shape. The following pages explore solutions for many of these situations.

One window is too close to a corner in this cozy living room. Simple window coverings—café curtains and swags without jabots—downplay the problem.

Skylight with Cellular Shade
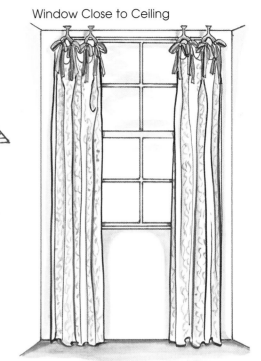

Window Close to Ceiling

Large Windows

Today, many homes feature a large window, such as a cathedral or geometric window, or several windows grouped together, such as a bay or Palladian window, dominating a wall. These windows are often an integral part of the architectural design of a room, providing access to beautiful views and allowing a maximum amount of light.

In such cases, large or grouped windows are left untreated or framed with a swag. More often, however, the placement of these windows means that neighbors can see in and that the light can be over-powering during certain times of the day. To find the best treatment for these openings, consider the following ideas.

Cathedral or Palladian Windows. A wall of windows is a common feature in a modern room, and one that can be

Cathedral Window with Curtains

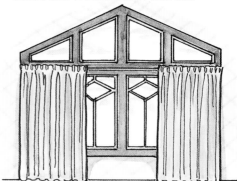

Palladian Window with Scarf

Angled Window with Shirred Curtain

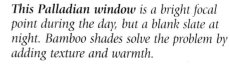

*This **Palladian window** is a bright focal point during the day, but a blank slate at night. Bamboo shades solve the problem by adding texture and warmth.*

daunting to treat. If lack of privacy is the problem, treat the lower half of a large window with curtains on a traverse or curtain rod and leave the transoms unadorned. Vertical blinds are another option, but they may look too severe for your decor. Try topping the blinds with a swag or a valance to soften the effect. Both of these arrangements show off the shape of a window while providing seclusion when needed.

Glare from the rising or setting sun can make a room uncomfortable. If harsh light comes through the transoms, you can completely cover the window with drapery. Keep in mind that treating the window in this way may overwhelm the room and look too staged. Another option is to hang a scarf across the transom, which often blocks enough light to make the room comfortable again and is less obtrusive. You can also treat each transom individually. Try shirred curtains anchored at the top and bottom of the window by rods, or vertical blinds and cellular shades in specialty shapes. A valance in a simple style, such as a chevron, can be hung on each transom. Remember, if the top half of a window is covered, usually the bottom half should also be treated to balance out the arrangement.

Bay or Bow Windows. When dealing with bay or bow windows, first decide how you want to treat them: individually or as a group. For individual treatments, try matching shades, blinds, or shutters, which create a clean, modern look. Or add tieback curtains for a softer style. A bow window requires a curved rod (which requires professional installation) or a wire hanging system. Instead of hanging curtains directly on the window frame, consider mounting the rod on the wall above the bow or bay.

On a bow window, *a pendant valance can be hung on a custom curved rod. The cellular shades provides light control for each window. The pale yellow palette picks up a color from this child's room, pulling the whole arrangement together.*

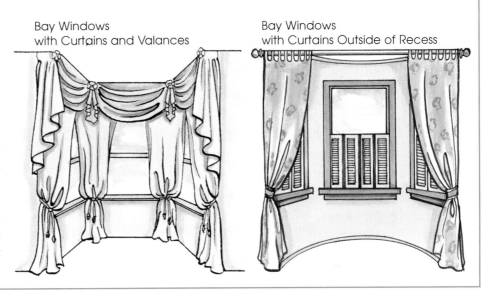

Bay Windows
with Curtains and Valances

Bay Windows
with Curtains Outside of Recess

Special Shapes

Windows with special shapes, such as ovals, ellipses, triangles, and arches, usually exist because they add architectural interest, both inside and outside of the house. Sometimes the best solution is no treatment at all. If you like the look of a bare window but sun glare is a problem, investigate professionally applied window film. This transparent covering filters out the majority of the sun's damaging ultraviolet rays while minimally darkening the glass.

Custom Shade on a Lancet Window

(Open)

(Closed)

Shaped Cornice on a Lancet Window

Scarf Swag on a Circular Window

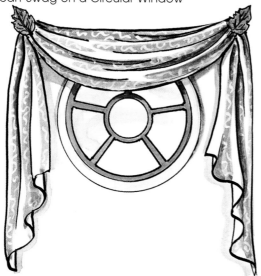

Shutters on an Elliptical Window

Sunburst Curtain on a Half-Round Window

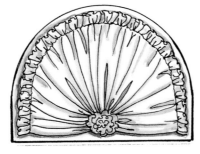

An arched window doesn't have to be completely covered with a treatment. Blue gingham curtains start at a natural break—just below the arch and in line with the room's plate rail.

Circles and Ovals. For complete coverage, stationary cellular shades are available in custom shapes. If privacy isn't an issue, a scarf swag draped over a pole or through sconces is a pleasing choice because the curve of the scarf echoes the curve of the window.

Half-rounds and Ellipses. Half-round and elliptical windows can be covered by a sunburst curtain, which is a rod-pocket curtain shirred on an arched rod. The lower edge is gathered into a rosette. Consider custom shutters and cellular shades, too.

Lancets. These Gothic-style arches can be difficult to treat. Try a shaped cornice with flanking curtains or specialty-shape cellular shade. A bottom-hung shade with a shaped hem is a custom item that provides maximum privacy. The shade is pulled up and attached by a tab to a peg or a hook.

Triangular Windows. Most triangular windows are left unadorned because they are usually placed above another window. However, strong sunlight can be a problem. Because of the angled shape, rod-pocket curtains are one of the few styles that work. Custom shutters, cellular shades, and vertical blinds are also attractive solutions. Remember that some of these treatments are stationary.

Arched Windows. You can either include or ignore the arch. If you leave it untreated, you can hang any curtain, swag, valance, shade, or blind on the lower portion of the window. Simply run the top of the treatment under the bottom of the arch. To cover the arch, try a floor-length scarf that is gathered and secured around the curve. Or install a sunburst curtain on the arch with shirred panels below. The headings of festoon shades can be shaped to fit, too.

A basic roll-up shade lets the shape of the window be the focal point of this bathroom instead of drawing attention to itself.

Shutters on a Triangular Window

Scarf Swag on an Arched Window

Balloon Shade on an Arched Window

No matter what type of glazed doors you have—French doors, sliding glass doors, or door-window combinations—the primary concern is leaving a clear passageway through the opening. If there is little wall space on either side of the opening, don't use a heavy fabric or a gathered curtain with a lot of fullness because it is too bulky and blocks access. Instead, choose a medium or light-weight fabric that stacks back tightly. If you are using a swag, check that it doesn't drape too low across the top where it can get caught in the door, particularly in the tracks of sliding glass doors.

Consider, too, which direction a door opens—in or out. There are more design options for an outward-opening door because a curtain is less likely to get caught in or block the door's operation. An inward-opening door often poses a problem; many curtain arrangements interfere with the movement of the door. Use treatments that can be secured above and below the glass on the door, such as some styles of shades, blinds, or shirred curtains on a pair of rods.

An arched French door features a butter-yellow scarf hung on intricate custom brackets. Notice that all parts of the arrangement clear the opening.

Cuffed Curtains & Vertical Blinds on a Sliding Glass Door

Valance & Curtains on a Sliding Glass Door

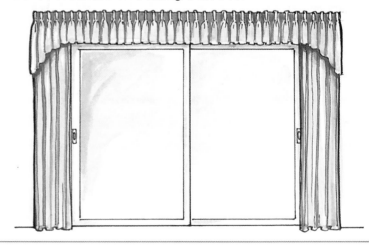

Blinds & Stagecoach Valance
on a French Door

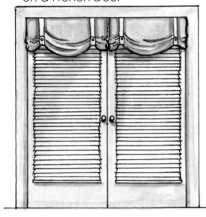

Curtains on a
French Door

Shades on a
Door-Window Combination

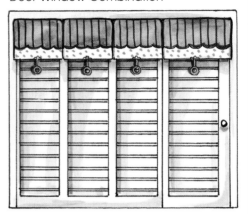

Sliding Glass Doors. Treatments that draw to one side, such as vertical blinds or curtains on a traverse rod, are the best options. Avoid any treatment that is mounted on the door itself because it will interfere with its operation.

French Doors. If the door opens out, a valance or cornice can be mounted at the top of the frame. If the door opens in, these headers are a possibility only if there is enough room to mount them on the wall above the door. Treatments that can be secured directly above and below the glass, and curtains that stack back tightly, work well. Shutters on tracks are a lovely choice, but they require substantial stack-back space.

Door-Window Combinations. You can treat this situation as one large unit, using the same guidelines as for sliding glass doors. For example, a valance or a cornice can unify the door and windows. Or you can dress each section individually with a series of matching elements. Try blinds on tracks or shades in tailored styles, such as roll-up or Roman ones.

This door-window combination is visually united by a colorful box-pleat valance with puddling sheer panels.

Dormer Windows

With dormer windows, you have the option of treating the window itself or the area outside of the recess—or both. Swing-out poles work best for hanging curtains on dormer windows because, when light is needed, the poles swivel so that the curtain is against the wall. Use a lightweight fabric so that the hardware isn't overloaded. If there is enough clearance, consider a roller shade. For a dormer with a sloped ceiling, such as in an attic, here is a theatrical solution: Hang a curtain rod on the wall outside of the recess. Secure the curtain with a second rod placed at the point where the ceiling and the wall meet.

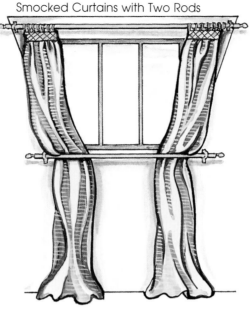
Smocked Curtains with Two Rods

For a dormer, *a valance and curtain are placed before the recess, creating a mock headboard above the bed.*

An extravagant, multilayered swag *fits neatly into this dormer's tight space and hangs well above the bathroom vanity, keeping the area clear for use.*

Rod-Pocket Curtains on Swivel Rods

Corner Windows

When dressing corner windows, unify them with matching fabrics or a treatment that visually joins the two windows together. Pull them together with a valance or a cornice—both treatments turn corners neatly. Curtains are also a good way to connect the windows. There are also a variety of tieback options. The panels can be tied back-to-back, or they can mirror each other. Formal window dressings involve a combination of both styles. Try balloon or cloud shades, too. Have the shade extend past the window slightly so that the corner is visually filled in; the fullness of the treatment helps to cover any gaps. Swags and jabots also bridge the gap. Cascade tails, in particular, visually complement each other in a corner.

Balloon Shades

Curtains in "Mirror" Arrangement

*A **corner window** is dressed in a swag-and-jabot arrangement. Jabots are good transitional elements for corners.*

Swags & Jabots with Tied-Back Curtains

CHAPTER 12

Make Your Own Curtains

Many of the window treatments popular today are combinations of individual elements that are easy to make, simply put together in a number of ways for great effects. Try making unlined curtains gathered on a rod, tabbed curtains with your choice of tab styles, or a scarf valance. Add some decorative details to your repertoire, such as a knotted rosette or a curtain cuff. If it's your first curtain project, choose according to your experience. Try to match it to your sewing knowledge, so whatever type of treatment you attempt, you won't feel overwhelmed. However, if you can sew a straight line with a sewing machine and know how to put in a hem using a slip stitch, you can create a variety of these decorating tricks.

Sheets are a great alternative to standard drapery fabric. Available in solid colors or in a variety of patterns, they are a fabric that's already seamed and hemmed for window treatments. Their sizes alone afford a source of material of greater widths than the average 54-inch-wide decorative fabric. Splurge on your favorite designer sheets or shop the sales for the best buys.

You can also experiment with creating some of the no-sew treatments. Seek out the various easy-to-use commercial products, such as iron-on seam tape, drapery tape, fabric glue, and pin-on and clip-on hooks.

*A **sheer scarf swag accented with knotted rosettes** gives a formal elegance to this kitchen bay window—a dramatic look that's simple and easy to create.*

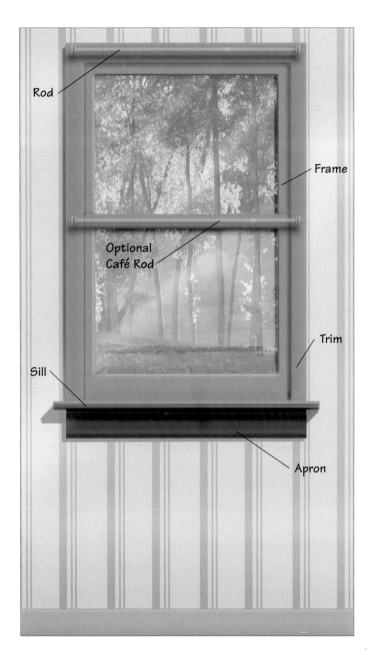

Rod

Frame

Optional
Café Rod

Trim

Sill

Apron

Measure twice, cut once. Insure success by starting your window treatment project with accurate measurements. You might even organize them in a notebook, adding photographs of styles you're considering, along with your favorite fabric swatches.

inside the window opening. Follow these three suggestions for greater accuracy: Use a sturdy, retractable metal measuring tape; ask someone to assist you; and use a step ladder to get the higher measurements. Be sure to double-check your figures.

INSIDE MOUNT

For a window treatment that you want to install inside the window opening, there are a few simple measurements to take: the length of the window from the top of the frame to the sill, and the inside width of the window. Because some windows are not perfectly plumb, take these measurements in three spots, and then working with the narrowest measurement, round up to the nearest $1/8$ inch. Do this for both the width and the length. Although this type of installation is more common for shades, blinds, or shutters, occasionally it is used for a curtain.

OUTSIDE MOUNT

Curtains, more often than shades, blinds, and shutters, are typically installed as an outside mount. Hardware, such as rods, poles, and brackets, are attached to the trim or wall outside the window opening. Decide where you want to install the curtain rod, and then measure the width from bracket to bracket. Add at least 3 inches to allow a center overlap. (If you are using a curved rod, add twice the number of inches the rod projects from the wall.)

Measuring Your Windows

The first step, in order to ensure that your chosen window treatment is a success, is to take a complete set of measurements for each window. The illustration above shows the parts of a standard double-hung window, which you should refer to as you read the instructions that follow for measuring for treatments requiring hardware mounted both outside and

Next, decide where you want the bottom of the curtain to fall: at the sill, the apron, or the floor; then measure down to that spot from the bottom of the rod, pole, or bracket. (If the curtain will hang from rings, measure from the base of the rings once they are installed on the rod or bracket.) Allow an extra 2 inches for the hardware.

Basic Techniques

Making a basic, unlined curtain is an easy first project for someone with a modest amount of sewing skills. The materials you'll need include fabric, fabric chalk or marker, coordinating thread, and shirring tape for a machine-stitched heading. You'll also need bent-handle shears, pins, needles, a yardstick (or a measuring tape), and a warm iron.

Trim off all selvages from fabric panels before you begin. The fabric for your curtain should measure two and a half to three times the desired finished width, plus 4 additional inches for 1-inch-wide double hems. Depending on the size of the fabric and your window, you may need more than one width (panel); you can use a partial width or even one on each side, if necessary.

Add double the desired width of the hem to the finished length of your curtain. (For example, add 2 inches for a 1-inch-wide hem.) If you're working with shirring tape, add twice the width of the shirring tape to the curtain's length.

First, mark and cut out the fabric. If there's more than one whole or partial width, lay them together, right sides facing; then join them using straight stitches. Don't forget to leave a ½-inch-wide seam allowance. Press the seams open. To clean-finish each seam allowance, place a row of zigzag stitches along each edge, or turn both seam allowances toward the seam line, and topstitch through the folded edges.

For a well-tailored look, your curtain should have neat, even hems. Pressing is an important step, as is mitering the corners. To do this, lay the fabric right side down. On both the sides and bottom, fold over half the hem allowance and press it; then fold over the other half, pressing it again. *The folded hems must be perfectly even.* Unfold the hems. Turn in each corner diagonally, folding it at the point where the inside creases of the two hems intersect. (See Figure 1.) Press the corner crease, and then fold it under itself halfway so that the point is tucked in. To reduce bulk, you could trim away this excess instead. Press it. Turn up the bottom hem twice. (See Figure 2.) Insert a small fabric weight into the hem, if desired. Turn up the side hem twice. Hand-sew (with a slip stitch) the mitered corner. Stitch both hems into place by machine or hand. (See Figure 3.) Press.

To finish the upper edge of the curtain, turn under the heading allowance once; then press. Turn under the heading allowance again. Press. Lay the heading tape a minimum of at least 1 inch down from the top edge; tuck it in at the sides, but leave the strings free. Pin the heading tape in place, and then machine-stitch it along the top and bottom edcges. On one side of the heading, knot the strings, tuck them under the tape, and then stitch that side closed. Pull the loose strings at the other side of the heading until the curtain is the correct width, and then knot them. Check the width of the curtain against your window, untie the knots, if necessary, to make adjustments, and re-knot and machine-stitch the side closed.

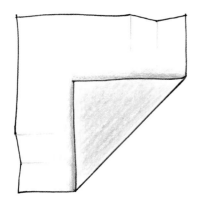

Figure 1: *Turn in corner so that its diagonal fold intersects the point where the bottom and side finished-edge creases meet.*

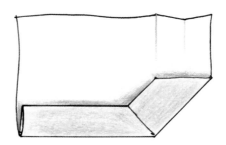

Figure 2: *Turn under the corner, trimming it if necessary to reduce bulk. Turn up the bottom hem allowance twice.*

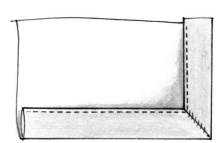

Figure 3: *Tuck in and smooth the edges of the mitered corner, and hand-sew it closed. Stitch the side and bottom hems in place.*

Rod-Pocket Curtains

In order to make a row of gathers at the top of a rod-pocket curtain, the fabric should be two and a half times the finished curtain width. Add double the depth of the rod pocket to the length's measurement. (See basic curtain panel, page 149.) For example, if you want a 3-inch-deep pocket, add 6 inches to the length. Turn the top edge over twice and stitch along the bottom fold. Insert the curtain rod into the pocket and gather.

To measure for a rod-pocket curtain with a ruffle, add four times the depth of the rod pocket. That figure should be added to the length of the basic curtain panel. Turn the top edge over twice, as directed at right. This top allowance should be deeper in order to provide for the ruffle. Stitch into place along the bottom fold. Measure up from the bottom to the center of the heading and stitch a second row across, creating two pockets. The top pocket becomes the ruffle; the bottom one holds the curtain rod.

Making a Rod-Pocket Curtain

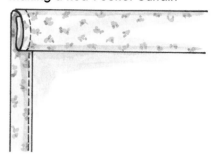

A Finished Rod-Pocket Curtain

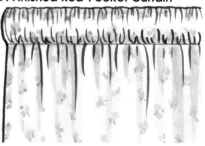

Making a Rod Pocket with Ruffle

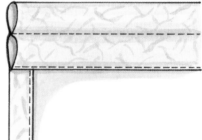

A Finished Rod Pocket with Ruffle

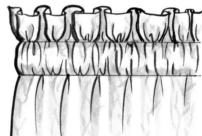

*A **simple ruffle** on this double-curtain treatment for a tall French window is part of the soft, straightforward French provincial look.*

Tabbed Curtains

Tabbed curtains are a great way to show off eye-catching drapery hardware. Start with a basic curtain panel. (See page 149.) Tabs are usually spaced from 5 to 8 inches apart. Divide the width of the finished curtain by the space desired between tabs. Then add one to that number for the number of tabs needed. For a 40-inch-wide curtain with 5 inches for tab spacing, divide 40 by 5, which equals 8. Add 1, for a total of nine tabs. For tab length, loop a measuring tape over the top of the curtain until your desired length. To this length add twice the width of the curtain header plus two seam allowances. Double the desired width of the tab and add a $1/2$ inch for the seam—a 3-inch-wide tab needs $6^1/_2$ inches of material.

Making the tabs. After cutting out the tabs, fold the fabric in half with the right sides facing, and stitch along the seam. Press the seam open and turn the tab right side out. Fold the tab in half, with the seam line facing in; then turn in the raw edges and pin the tab at the marking on the top edge of the curtain. To secure the tab, stitch an X inside a rectangle. (See the illustration at right.)

Other variations include bow ties and button tabs. To make a bow tie, fold a length of ribbon in half. Stitch that center point to the hem on the back of the curtain. For button tabs, follow the directions for regular tabs, as above. Hand-sew one end closed, form a buttonhole in that end, and attach the other end of the tab to the curtain. Attach buttons on the curtain at the same intervals used for the tabs.

Making a Tab Curtain

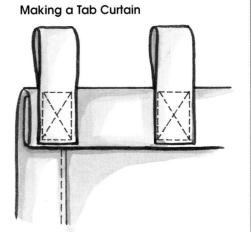

Making a Bow-Tie Heading

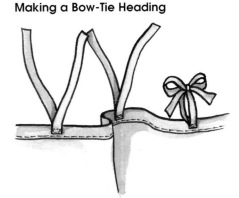

Making a Button Tab

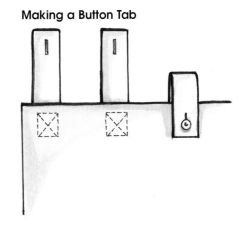

Tab-style curtains show off the decorative hardware as part of the treatment's overall design.

A Simple Scarf

Decide on the location of the holdbacks, and measure the distance between them. Measure how far down from the holdbacks you want the tails to fall. Add together the distance between the holdbacks plus twice the length of the tail. Add 1 inch for seam allowances. This is the cutting length of your fabric. The cutting width is the width of your fabric panel after trimming the selvages.

Based on the measurements, cut a rectangle of fabric. Fold each end in to meet at center of fabric; crease each fold. Unfold; mark a diagonal line from each upper corner down to the crease at the lower edge. Cut along these lines, and use this as a pattern for cutting out the lining. Right sides facing, sew fabrics together, leaving a small opening. Turn fabrics right side out. Slip stitch opening closed; press. Fold scarf into accordion pleats, and drape over the holdbacks.

A graceful scarf valance on this window sets a mood of casual formality.

Making a Simple Scarf

Step 1. Cut out the fabric.

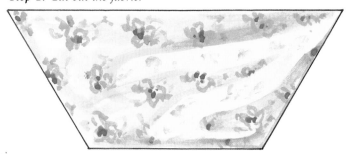

Step 2. Make accordion pleats.

Step 3. Install the finished scarf over the holdbacks.

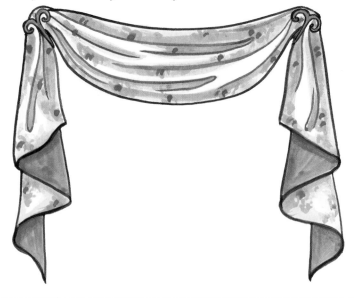

Decorative Details

Here are two quick projects. The first is an easy rosette detail that you can make from a short length of fabric and add to a simple scarf. The second is a cuff, used to create an attractive layered effect on tab and bow-tie curtains.

Making a Knotted Rosette

Easy Rosette: Knot a length of fabric on top of your wrist and leave the ends hanging. (See Step 1.) Then tie the two ends together *below* your wrist and tighten. (See Step 2.) Last, slip the material off your hand and tighten the rosette a bit more, but don't overdo it. (See Step 3.) Leave some fullness in the rosette. Do this for each rosette. Lightweight materials, such as lace and voiles, work best for this detail.

Position a rosette on a scarf valance at the point where two windows meet to create a lush accent. Tuck in the ends.

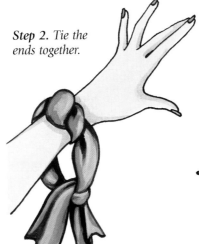

Step 1. Knot the fabric loosely.

Step 2. Tie the ends together.

Step 3. Fluff the rosette.

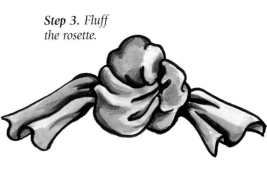

Making a Curtain Cuff

Charming Cuff: The measurement for the cuff is double its depth plus $1/2$ inch for the fold. If you want a 6-inch-deep cuff, measure 6 inches plus 6 inches plus $1/2$ inch for the fold, which equals $12\frac{1}{2}$ inches. Add this total to the length of the basic curtain panel. (See page 149.)

At the top of the curtain, make a $1/2$-inch fold and secure. Fold fabric down double the distance of the cuff. Then fold up half of material. Baste the top edge of the cuff into place. Slip stitch or machine-stitch the cuff in place; remove basting. Add tabs or bow ties. (See page 151.)

Step 1. Fold the fabric.

Step 2. Stitch the cuff.

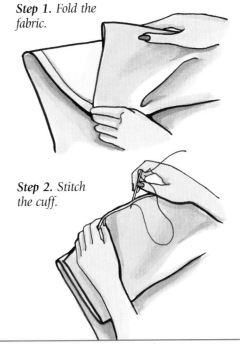

A curtain cuff is used here for fullness at the top of the curtain in the place of a conventional valance

Appendix

Templates are an easy way to see how different styles look on a particular window. Simply photocopy, enlarge, or color them to try out different looks. Mix and match until you find an arrangement that you like.

DOUBLE-HUNG AND CASEMENT WINDOW TEMPLATES

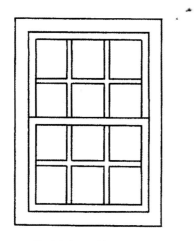

Double-hung Window

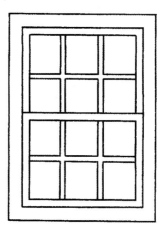

Double-hung Window

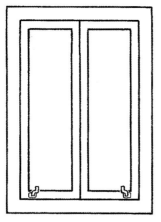

Casement Window

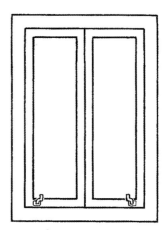

Casement Window

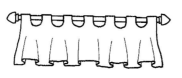

Tab Valance

Cornice

DOUBLE-HUNG AND CASEMENT WINDOW TEMPLATES

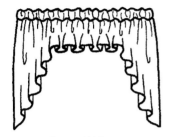

Tapered Valance

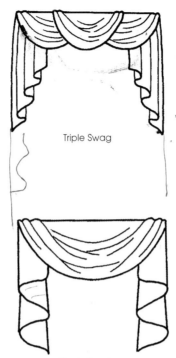

Triple Swag

Triple Swag

Double Swag

Single Swag

Single Swag

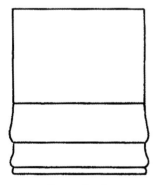

Roman Shade

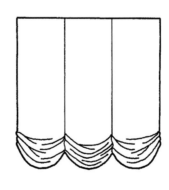

Balloon Shade

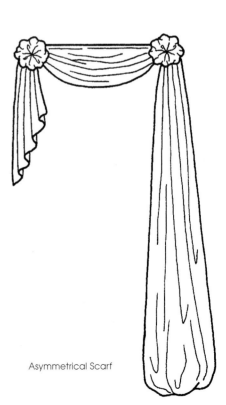

Asymmetrical Scarf

Curtain Rod

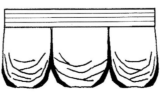

Balloon Valance

DOUBLE-HUNG AND CASEMENT WINDOW TEMPLATES CONT'D

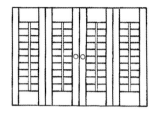

Shutters

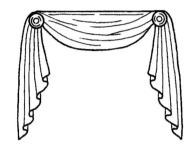

Scarf

Blinds

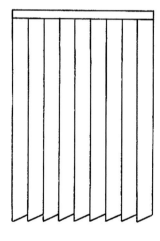

Vertical Blinds

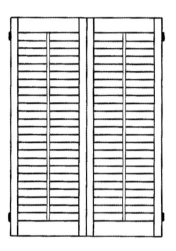

Plantation Shutters

Tab Café Curtains

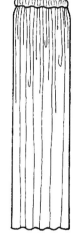

Rod-pocket Curtains

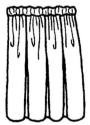

Café Curtains

PICTURE WINDOW TEMPLATES

Picture Window

Tab Valance

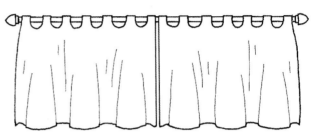

Tab Café Curtains

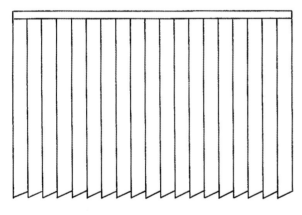

Vertical Blinds

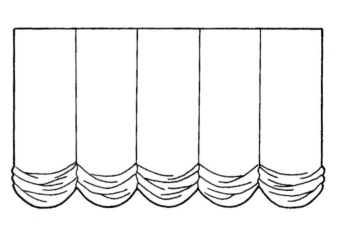

Balloon Shade

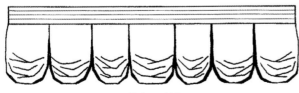

Balloon Valance

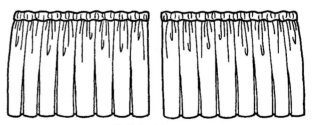

Café Curtains

PICTURE WINDOW TEMPLATES

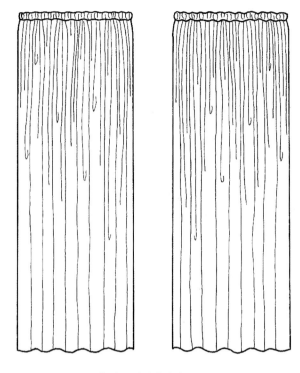

Rod-pocket Curtains

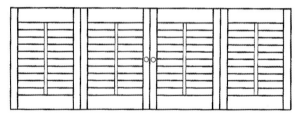

Café Shutters

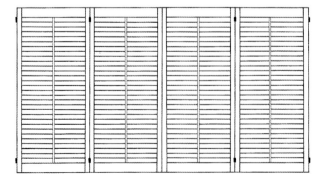

Plantation Shutters

BOW WINDOW TEMPLATES

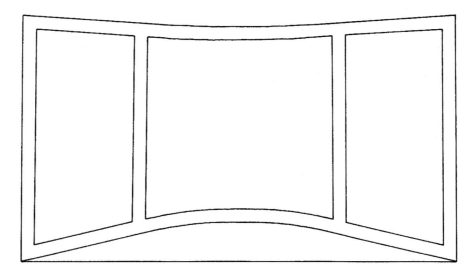

Bow Window

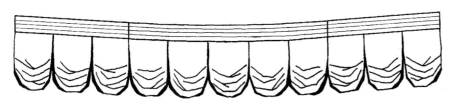

Balloon Valance

Tab Valance

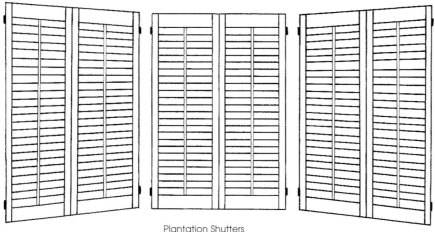

Plantation Shutters

BOW WINDOW TEMPLATES

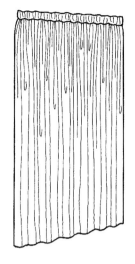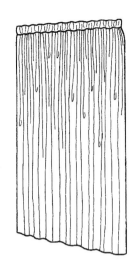

Rod-pocket Curtains

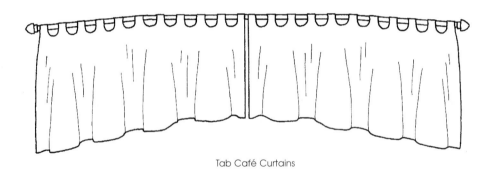

Tab Café Curtains

BAY WINDOW TEMPLATES

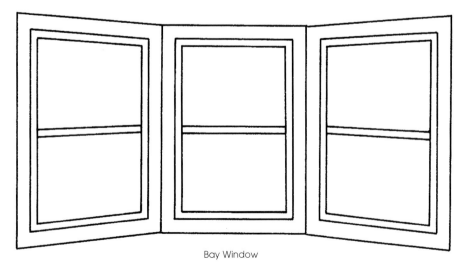

Bay Window

BAY WINDOW TEMPLATES

Rod-pocket Curtains

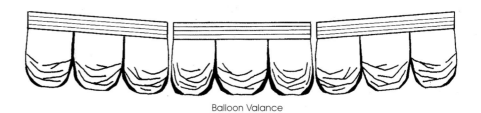

Balloon Valance

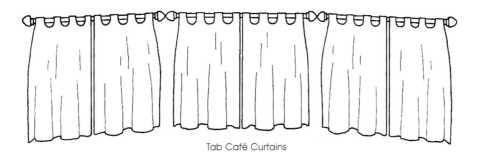

Tab Café Curtains

BAY WINDOW TEMPLATES

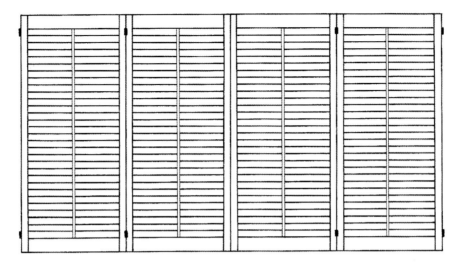

Plantation Shutters

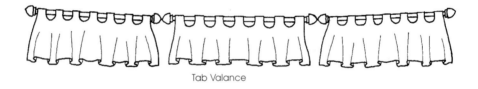

Tab Valance

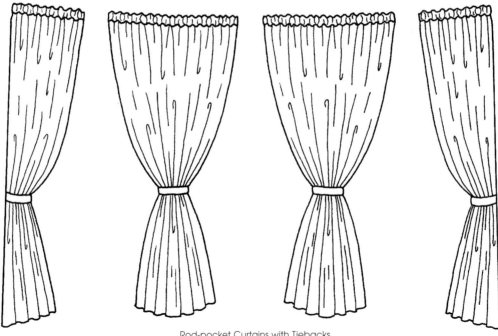

Rod-pocket Curtains with Tiebacks

BAY WINDOW TEMPLATES

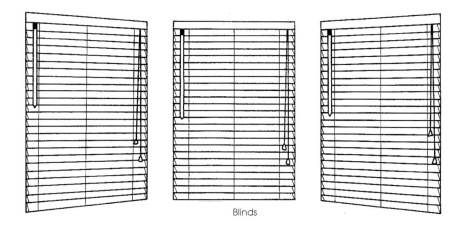

Blinds

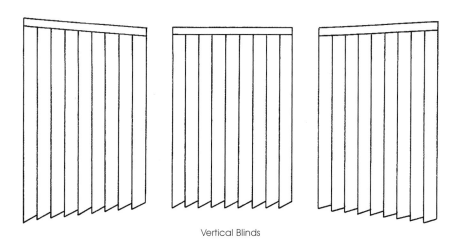

Vertical Blinds

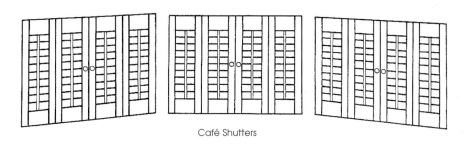

Café Shutters

LARGE AND SMALL ARCH TEMPLATES

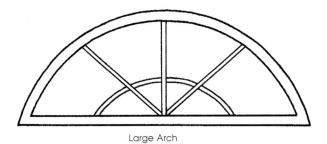
Large Arch

Scarf

Large Shutter

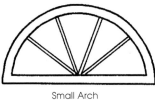
Small Arch

Sunburst Curtain

Small Shutter

SLIDING GLASS DOOR & FRENCH DOOR TEMPLATES

Sliding Glass Door

French Door

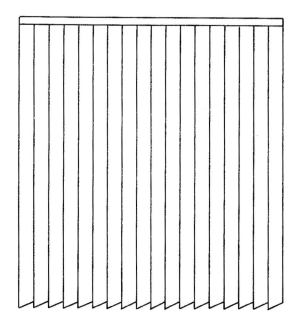

Vertical Blinds

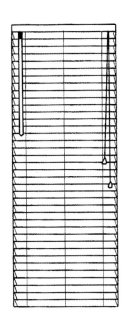

Blinds (French Door Only)

SLIDING GLASS DOOR, FRENCH DOOR, & CATHEDRAL DOOR TEMPLATES CONT'D

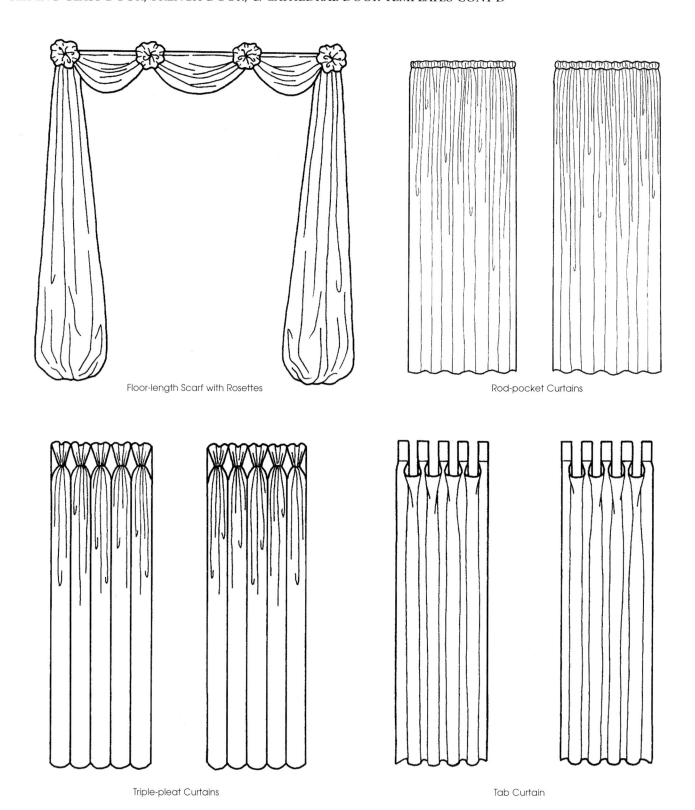

Floor-length Scarf with Rosettes

Rod-pocket Curtains

Triple-pleat Curtains

Tab Curtain

CATHEDRAL DOOR TEMPLATES

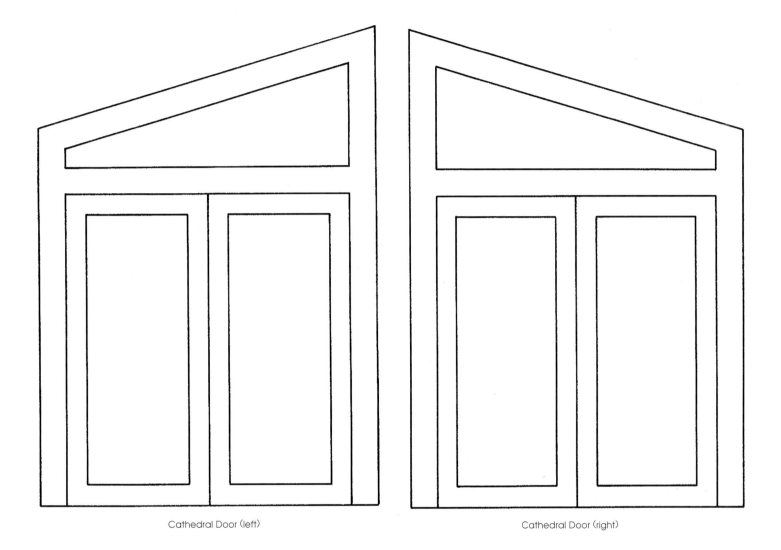

Cathedral Door (left)   Cathedral Door (right)

Vertical Blinds (Cathedral Doors Only)

SLIDING GLASS DOOR, FRENCH DOOR, & CATHEDRAL DOOR TEMPLATES CONT'D

Rod-pocket Curtains with Tiebacks

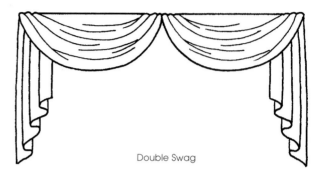

Double Swag

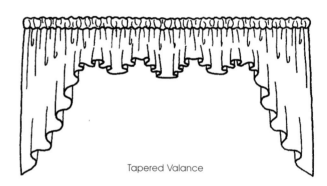

Tapered Valance

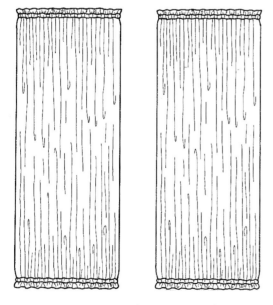

Shirred Curtains (French Door Only)

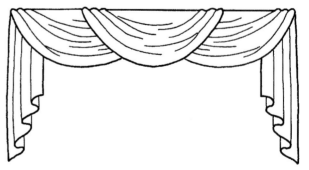

Triple Swag

SLIDING GLASS DOOR, FRENCH DOOR, & CATHEDRAL DOOR TEMPLATES CONT'D

Triple Swag

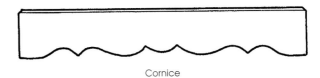

Cornice

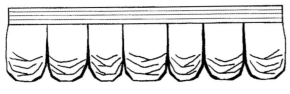

Balloon Valance

Curtain Rod

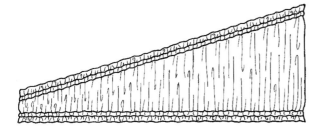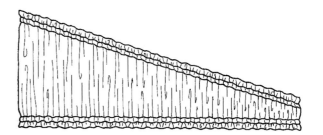

Shirred Curtains (Cathedral Doors Only)

Glossary

Austrian Shade: An opulent-style shade that hangs in cascading scallops from top to bottom, often made of a sheer or lacy fabric. It is raised by a cord system.

Awning Window: Wide, horizontal sashes that open outward.

Balloon Shade: A fabric shade that falls in full blousy folds at the bottom, raised by a cord system.

Bay Window: Three or more windows set at an angle in a recessed area.

Bow Window: A curved bay window.

Box Pleats: Two folds turned toward each other, creating a flat-fronted pleat.

Brackets: Hardware attached to the window to support the curtain rod or pole.

Brocade: A weighty, typically formal, fabric in silk, cotton, wool or combination. It is distinguished by a raised, often floral, design in a Jacquard weave.

Buckram: A coarse fabric, stiffened with glue, used to give body and shape to curtain headings.

Cased Heading: Fabric folded over and anchored with a row of stitching, left open at both ends to hold a curtain rod.

Casement Window: A vertical window that opens in or out, often operated with a crank mechanism.

Chintz: A cotton fabric that is coated with a resin to give it a sheen, often in a floral or other overall print.

Clerestory Window: A window set near the ceiling.

Cornice: A projecting, decorative box installed above a window, designed to hide a curtain rod.

Damask: A Jacquard-weave material made of cotton, silk, wool, or a combination with a satin, raised design. Widely used for draperies.

Dormer Window: A projecting window set into the slope of a roof. In the interior, often a bedroom or attic, the window sits within the resulting alcove-like space.

Double-hung Window: The most common type, consisting of two sashes, one atop the other, which slide up and down to open and close.

Face Fabric: The main, outer fabric used in a window treatment.

Finial: The decorative ends of a curtain rod or pole.

Flemish Heading: A pleat that is stuffed with batting to create a puffed appearance; also called a *Goblet Pleat Heading*.

French Door: A door, typically with 12 divided panes of glass, used alone or in pairs. It is also used as a fixed window.

Goblet Pleat: See *Flemish Heading*.

Heading: The horizontal area at the top of a curtain. Its style determines how a curtain hangs.

Holdback: Curtain hardware made of metal, wood, or glass. It is attached to the wall near the edge of the window, and used in place of a fabric tieback.

Interlining: Made of lightweight, opaque fabric, it is used between the curtain fabric and the lining to add body or to block light.

Jabot: The vertical tail that complements a swag in a swag-and-jabot treatment.

Jacquard: A type of fabric and weave; also the name of a loom, named after its inventor, which revolutionized weaving by using punched cards that produced intricate designs.

Lambrequin: A painted board or stiffened fabric that surrounds the top and side of a window or a door. Historically, it also was drapery that hung from a shelf, such as a mantel.

Lining: Added to the primary window fabric for body and a visually unified exterior appearance; it also helps to control light, air, and dust that filters in from the window.

Miter: A sewing technique for creating a flat corner where two hemmed edges meet.

Moiré: A fabric finish on silk or acetate, intended to resemble water marking. The fabric must be dry-cleaned.

Muslin: Ranging from coarse to fine, a plain-weave cotton; also called *voile*.

Palladian Window: A group of three windows with an arch over the center unit.

Pattern Matching: To align a repeating pattern when joining together two pieces of fabric.

Piping: An trim edging made of bias-cut fabric encasing cording, which is sewn onto the side, top, and bottom edges of a curtain.

Pleater Hooks: Metal hooks that are inserted into pleating tape to create pleats.

Pleating Tape: A cotton or nylon strip with strings, which are drawn to make various styles of pleats. It is stitched onto the back of a curtain heading, and pleater hooks are inserted into ready-made pockets.

Return: The distance from the front of a rod to the wall or where the brackets are attached.

Rod: Metal or wood hardware that supports curtain fabric; also called a pole.

Roman Shade: Made of fabric, it hangs in straight, flat horizontal folds when open. It is operated by pulling a cord that is threaded through rings attached to a fabric tape sewn to the reverse side of the face fabric or the lining.

Stackback: The space along the sides of a window taken up by a curtain when open.

Swag: The center drape of fabric in a swag-and-jabot treatment, which can have a deep or shallow drop.

Taffeta: A silk-and-acetate weave that appears shiny and maintains shape. It is used for formal curtains and borders.

Tail: A common term for jabot, the vertical lengths of fabric that complement a swag on either side of a window.

Tieback: A fabric strip or cord used to hold curtains open; also a style of curtain.

Toile de Jouy: An eighteenth-century print design of pastoral scenes on cotton or linen, printed in one color on a white background; first produced in Jouy, France.

Valance: A short length of fabric that hangs along the top of a window, with or without a curtain underneath.

Voile: See *Muslin.*

Index

A
Air flow, 15
Angled double tie, 54
Appliquéd borders, 116
Arched windows, 23, 141
Architecture, observing, 16
Austrian shade, 75
Austrian valance, 94

B
Balance, 28-29
Balloon shade, 74-75
Balloon valance, 94
Banner valance, 96
Basket weave, 104
Bay windows, 139
Bell-pleat valance, 95
Below-sill length, 51-52
Bishop's sleeve, 54
Blackout lining, 58
Blinds, 18, 76
    matchstick, 77
    materials for, 76
    plastic, 77
    Venetian, 78
    vertical, 78-79
    wood-slat, 78
    woven, 77
Borders, 116
    appliquéd, 116
    Jacquard, 120
Bow tiebacks, 114, 115
Bow windows, 22, 139
Box cornices, 100
Box pleat, 62
Braided tiebacks, 114, 115
Brocade, 105
Brush fringe, 121
Budget, 44-47
Bunched heading, 61
Butterfly pleat, 62
Butterfly-pleat valance, 95

C
Café curtain, 50
Café shutter, 82
Cambric, 105
Campaign fringe, 121
Cane blinds, 76
Canvas, 105
Cartridge pleat, 95
Cartridge pleat heading, 63
Cascade jabot, 88
Cascade shades, 69, 73
Casement curtain, 56
Casement windows, 16, 22
Cathedral windows, 23, 138-39
Ceiling-mounted rods, 126

Cellular shades, 71
Center tie, 54
Chintz, 105
Choux, 118
Circles and ovals, 141
Clerestory window, 22
Cloud shade, 75
Cloud valance, 94
Color, 34
Concealed tieback holder, 130
Concealed-track rod, 127
Continental rod, 126
Cool colors, 34
Cording, 120
Cording system, 125
Corner windows, 145
Cornices, 56, 98-100
    box, 100
    pendant, 99
    shaped, 99
Cotton duck, 105
Crescent tiebacks, 114
Crewel, 105
Curtain cuff, 153
Curtain rods, 126-27
Curtains, 49, 50
    café, 50
    casement, 56
    dressing, 55
    floor-length, 52-53
    headings, 59-65
    length of, 51-54
    lined, 58-59
    making your own, 147-53
    rod pocket, 150
    sill-length, 51
    tabbed, 151
    tieback positions for, 54
    tiered, 50
    types of, 50
    unlined, 58
Curtain weight, 52
Curved lines, 28

D
Damask, 105
Decor, identifying, 31-37
Decorative embellishments, 111-21
Decorative role of
    window treatments, 18
Decorative trims, 70
Diagonal lines, 28
Door-window combinations, 143
Dormer windows, 144
Double-hung windows, 16, 22
Double ruffle, 116
Double-track rod, 127
Draped pole, 91

Draperies, 49
Drapery hardware, 123-31
Drapery pins, 131
Dressing, 55

E
Ellipses, 141
Elliptical window, 23

F
Fabric blinds, 76
Fabric-insert shutter, 83
Fabric rose, 119
Fabrics, 36
    choosing, 103-9
    draping ability, 109
    selecting, 108-9
Fabric tiebacks, 115
Fan-edge braid, 121
Fan pleats, 62
Fan shades, 73
Fan swag, 88
Federal valance, 97
Festoon shades, 74
Finials, 129
Flat braid, 120
Flemish heading, 63
Floor-length curtain, 52-53
Fluted jabot, 89
Folds, 62
Form, 14-18
French doors, 17, 143
Fringe, 121
Frog tassel, 117
Function, 14-18

G
Galloon, 120
Gathered headings, 61
Gathered valances, 97
Gimp, 120
Gingham, 105
Glazed doors, 142-43
Goblet pleat, 63

H
Half-rounds, 141
Hardware
    choosing, 124-25
    operating controls, 125
    for valances, 93, 96
Harmony, 29
Headings
    bunched, 61
    Flemish, 63
    gathered, 61
    looped, 64

    pierced, 65
    plain, 65
    pleated, 62-63
    rod-pocket, 60
    rod sleeve, 60-61
    smocked, 62
    tabbed, 64
    tied, 64
Headrail, 124-25
Holdbacks, 130
Horizontal lines, 28

I
Inside mount
    measuring blinds for, 69
    measuring windows for, 148-49
Interlinings, 58

J
Jabots, 86, 88-89
    fluted, 89
    pipe, 89
Jacquard border, 120
Jacquard weave, 104
Jalousie window, 22

K
Key tassel, 117
Knife-pleated rosette, 119
Knotted rosette, 153
Knotted tiebacks, 114, 115

L
Lace, 105
Lambrequins, 56, 101
Lancets, 141
Lifestyle, 40-44
    external appearances in, 42
    family members in, 42-43
    location in, 41-42
    maintenance in, 44
    personal preference in, 40-41
    pets in, 43-44
Lined curtains, 58-59
Linen, 105
Lining, 57-58, 58
Looped fringe, 121
Looped heading, 64
Louvers, 81

M
Maltese cross, 118
Matchstick blinds, 77
Metal blinds, 76
Metal poles, 129
Miniblind, 78
Mismatched windows, 136
Mitered corner, making, 149

Moiré, 106
Monochromatic color schemes, 34
Muslin, 106

N
North-facing rooms, 16-17

O
Oval window, 23
Organdy, 106
Outside mount
    measuring blinds for, 69
    measuring windows for, 148-49
Overdraperies, 56-57

P
Palladian windows, 21, 22, 138-39
Panel shutter, 83
Paper blinds, 76
Passementerie, 111, 112-13
Patterns, 35-36
    mixing, 107-8
Pencil pleats, 62, 115
Pendant cornice, 99
Pets, 43-44
Picot braid, 120
Picture window, 22
Pierced heading, 65
Pile weave, 104
Pipe jabot, 89
Piping, 121
Plain heading, 65
Plain weave, 104
Plantation shutter, 82
Plastic blinds, 76, 77
Pleated-and-gathered valance, 95
Pleated headings, 62-63
Pleated ruffle, 116
Pleated shades, 71
Pleated tiebacks, 114
Pleated valances, 95
Pleats
    box, 62
    butterfly, 62
    cartridge, 63
    fan, 62
    goblet, 63
    triple, 62
Poles
    metal, 129
    wooden, 128
Prairie points, 116
Problem solving, 133-45
Professional, hiring, 47
Proportions, 26-29, 113, 136
Puddling, 53, 91
Puff valance, 94

R
Rattan shades, 67
Rhythm, 29
Ribbed weave, 104
Rod-pocket curtains, 150

Rod-pocket heading, 60
Rods
    ceiling-mounted, 126
    concealed-track, 127
    continental, 126
    curtain, 126-27
    double-track, 127
    standard traverse, 126
    swivel, 127
    tension, 126
    track-and-valance, 127
    wire, 127
Rod sleeve, 60-61
Roller shades, 69, 70, 72
Roll-up shade, 73
Roman shades, 69, 73
Rosette, 117, 153
    knife-pleated, 119
    knotted, 153
    ruffle, 119
Ruffled tiebacks, 114
Ruffle rosette, 119
Ruffles, 116
    double, 116
    pleated, 116

S
Satin, 107
Satin weave, 104
Scale, 113
Scarf swags, 90-91
Scarf valance, 152
Screen, Shoji, 83
Shades, 18, 68-69
    Austrian, 75
    balloon, 74-75
    cascade, 69, 73
    cellular, 71
    fan, 73
    festoon, 74
    mounting of, 68-69
    pleated, 71
    rattan, 66
    roller, 69, 72
    rollers, 70
    roll-up, 73
    roman, 69, 73
    tailed balloon, 75
Shading, window, 79
Shaped cornices, 99
Shaped tiebacks, 115
Shoji screen, 83
Shutters, 18, 80-81
    café, 82
    fabric-insert, 83
    materials, 81
    panel, 83
    plantation, 82
    vertical-louver, 82
Sight lines, 15
Silk, 107
Sill-length curtain, 51
Skirting, 74-75

Skylights, 137
Sliding glass doors, 143
Sliding window, 22
Smocked heading, 62
Spiral, 89
Split headrail, 125
Stack-back, 49
Standard traverse rod, 126
Stiffeners and tapes, 63
Swag holder, 131
Swags, 86-91
    fan, 88
    scarf, 90-91
Swivel rod, 127

T
Tabbed curtains, 151
Tabbed heading, 64
Tabbed valances, 96
Tabs, 64
Taffeta, 107
Tailed balloon shade, 75
Tapestry, 107
Tasseled fringe, 121
Tassels, 117
    frog, 117
    key, 117
    rosette, 117
Tension rod, 126
Texture, 36
Tiebacks, 114-15
    fabric, 115
    position of, 54
    shaped, 115
Tied heading, 64
Tiered curtains, 50
Toile de Jouy, 107
Track-and-valance rod, 127
Trapezoidal window, 23
Triangular windows, 23, 141
Trimmings, 120-21
Triple pleat, 62
Triple-pleat valances, 95
Twill weave, 104

U
Unlined curtains, 58

V
Valances, 56, 92-97
    Austrian, 94
    balloon, 94
    banner, 96
    bell-pleat, 95
    butterfly-pleat, 95
    cartridge-pleat, 95
    cloud, 94
    Federal, 97
    gathered, 97
    hardware for, 93
    pleated, 95
    pleated-and-gathered, 95
    proportion of, 92

puff, 94
    scarf, 152
    style of, 93
    tabbed, 96
    triple-pleat, 95
Velvet, 107
Venetian blind, 78
Ventilation, 15
Vertical blind, 78-79
Vertical lines, 28
Vertical-louver shutter, 82
Vinyl blinds, 76
Vinyl shutters, 81

W
Warm colors, 34
Welting, 121
Windows
    assessing your, 23-26
    designs for difficult, 134-45
    measuring your, 148-49
    mismatched, 136
    with special shapes, 140-41
    types of, 22-23
    arched, 23, 141
    bay, 139
    bow, 22, 139
    casement, 16, 22
    cathedral, 23, 138-39
    clerestory, 22
    corner, 145
    dormer, 144
    double-hung, 16, 22
    elliptical, 23
    jalousie, 22
    oval, 23
    palladian, 138-39
    picture, 22
    sliding, 22
    trapezoidal, 23
    triangular, 23, 141
Window shading, 79
Window style
    assessing needs, 32-34
    identifying, 21-29
    proportion, 26-29
Window treatments
    color of, 34
    decorative role of, 18
    fabrics for, 104-9
    formal versus informal, 56-58
    patterns for, 35-36, 107-8
    planning, in stages, 46
    practical role of, 16-18
    problem solving with, 133-45
    purpose of, 12
    role of, 12-18
    selecting right, 9-11
    texture of, 36
Wire rod, 127
Wood crown, 99
Wooden poles, 128
Wood shutters, 81
Wood-slat blind, 78
Woven blinds, 77

Photography Credits

Opening

p. 1: *Photographer:* Mark Lohman. **p. 2:** *Photographer:* Melabee M Miller. **p. 5:** *Photographer:* Tria Giovan.

Introduction

pp. 8-9: *Photographer:* Sam Gray; *Designer:* Kathy Venier. **p. 10:** *Photographer:* Tria Giovan. **p. 10:** *Photographer:* Melabee M Miller; *Designers:* Rosemarie Cicio, Susan Rosenthal. **p. 11:** *Photographer:* Mark Lohman. **p. 11:** *Photographer:* Gordon Beall. **p. 11:** *Photographers:* Steve Gross & Susan Daley.

Chapter One

pp. 12-14: *Photographer:* Mark Lohman. **p. 15:** *Photographer:* Tria Giovan. **p. 16:** *Photographer:* Nancy Hill; *Designer:* Karyne Johnson, Panache Interiors **p. 17:** *Photographer (top):* Bob Greenspan; *Stylist:* Susan Andrews. *Photographer (bottom):* Mark Lohman. **p. 18:** *Photographer:* Tria Giovan. **pp. 18-19:** *Photographer:* Sam Gray. **p. 19:** *Photographer:* Gordon Beall.

Chapter Two

pp. 20-21: *Photographer:* Nancy Hill; *Designer:* Diana Sawicki. **p. 22** *Photographer:* davidduncanlivingston.com. **p. 23:** *Photographer:* Woody Cady. **p. 24:** *Photographer:* davidduncanlivingston.com. **p. 25:** *Photographer (top):* davidduncanlivingston.com. *Photographer (bottom):* Mark Lohman; *Designer:* Janet Lohman. **p. 26:** *Photographer:* Jessie Walker. **p. 27:** *Photographer (top):* Nancy Hill; *Designer:* Karyne Johnson, Panache Interiors. *Photographer (bottom):* Sam Gray. **p. 28:** *Photographer:* Sam Gray; *Designer:* Kathy Venier. **p. 29:** *Photographer:* davidduncanlivingston.com.

Chapter Three

pp. 30-31: *Photographer:* Nancy Hill; *Designer:* Sheridan Interiors. **p. 32:** *Photographer:* Tria Giovan. **p. 33:** *Photographer:* Melabee M Miller; *Designer:* Jeffery Scott Queripel. **p. 34:** *Photographer:* davidduncanlivingston.com. **pp. 34-35:** *Photographer:* Mark Lohman **p. 35:** *Photographer:* Tria Giovan. **p. 36:** *Photographer:* Mark Lohman; *Designer:* Janet Lohman. **p. 37:** *Photographer:* Mark Lohman.

Chapter Four

pp. 38-39: *Photographer:* davidduncanlivingston.com. **p. 40:** *Photographer:* Tria Giovan. **p. 41:** *Photographer (left):* Sam Gray; *Designer:* Bierly-Drake. *Photographer (right):* Mark Lohman; *Designer:* Janet Lohman. **p: 42:** *Photographer:* Mark Lohman. **p. 43:** *Photographer:* davidduncanlivingston.com. **p. 44:** *Photographer:* davidduncanlivingston.com. **p. 45:** *Photographer:* Melabee M Miller; *Designer:* Deborah Leamann. **p. 46:** *Photographer:* Mark Lohman; *Designer:* Janet Lohman. **p. 47:** *Photographer:* Mark Lohman.

Chapter Five

pp. 48-49: *Photographer:* Anne Gummerson. **p. 50:** *Photographer:* davidduncanlivingston.com. **p. 51:** *Photographer:* Melabee M Miller; *Designer:* Susan Rosenthal. **p. 52:** *Photographer:* Mark Lohman. **p. 53:** *Photographer:* Nancy Hill/Courtesy of *House Beautiful.* **pp. 56-58:** *Photographer:* Mark Lohman. **p. 59:** *Photographer:* Tria Giovan. **p. 61:** *Photographer:* davidduncanlivingston.com. **p. 63:** *Photographer:* Mark Samu. **p. 64:** Photograph courtesy of Country Curtains. **p. 65:** *Photographer:* Mark Samu.

Chapter Six

pp. 66-67: *Photographer:* davidduncanlivingston.com. **pp. 68 & 71:** *Photographer:* Tria Giovan. **p. 72:** *Photographer:* Bob Greenspan; *Stylist:* Susan Andrews. **p. 73:** *Photographer:* Tria Giovan. **p. 74:** *Photographer:* Mark Lohman. **p. 75:** *Photographer:* Tria Giovan. **p. 76:** *Photographer:* davidduncanlivingston.com. **p.77:** *Photographer:* Mark Lohman. **p. 78:** *Photographer:* davidduncanlivingston.com. **p. 79:** *Photographer:* Alan Shortall. **p. 80:** *Photographer:* Mark Lohman. **pp. 81-82:** *Photographer:* Gordon Beall. **p. 83:** *Photographer:* Anne Gummerson.

Chapter Seven

pp. 84-85: *Photographer:* Mark Lohman; *Designer:* Kathryne Dahlman, Kathryne Designs. **p. 86:** *Photographer:* Mark Lohman; *Designer:* Janet Lohman. **p. 87:** *Photographer:* davidduncanlivingston.com. **p. 88:** *Photographer:* Mark Lohman; *Designer:* Kathryne Dahlman, Kathryne Designs. **p. 89:** *Photographer:* Melabee M Miller; *Designer:* Suzanne S. Curtis, ASID. **p. 90:** *Photographers:* Steve Gross & Susan Daley. **p. 91:** *Photographer:* Melabee M Miller; *Designer:* Geraldine Kaupp. **pp. 92-93:** *Photographer:* Nancy Hill; *Designer:* Karyne Johnson/Panache Interiors. **p. 93:** *Photographer:* Steven Mays. **p. 94:** *Photographer:* Mark Lohman; *Designer:* Kathryne Dahlman, Kathryne Designs. **p. 95:** *Photographer:* Melabee M Miller; *Designer:* Jeffery Scott Queripel. **p. 96:** *Photographer:* Tria Giovan. **p. 97:** *Photographer:* Nancy Hill **pp. 98-100:** *Photographer:* Tria Giovan. **p. 101:** *Photographer:* Al Teufen.